GOLF WEST™

PUBLISHED BY

JAY D. JENKS & STEVEN L. WALKER

And Golf West Publishing, Inc. Associate Publishers: Brian R. Graff and
Lori Shelton-Jenks Photography: All photographs created by Jay D. Jenks
and Steven L. Walker except where otherwise noted. Creative Directors:
Steven L. Walker and Jay D. Jenks. Text: Steven L. Walker, Jay D. Jenks,
Brian R. Graff and a host of clients and friends. Electronic Pre-Press:
Golf & Travel and Camelback Design Group, Inc.'s Scottsdale, Arizona
and San Clemente, California studios. Counsel: Joseph A. Shuff III.

Previous Pages: The 15th hole at Cypress Point, California.

This Page: Sunset at Carmel by the Sea, California.

Requests for additional information should be made to Golf West
Publishing, 22211 North Los Caballos Drive, Scottsdale, Arizona
85255 USA. Telephone: 480-948-4723 Facsimile: 480-483-8430
E-mail: Information@GolfandTravel.com or visit us on the Internet at
www.GolfandTravel.com.

Printed in South Korea
Library of Congress Control Number: 2002096383
International Standard Book Number: 1-879924-33-1
Published in the United States of America

GOLF WEST™

A PHOTOGRAPHIC JOURNEY OF THE WESTERN WORLD

BY

JAY D. JENKS & STEVEN L. WALKER

TABLE OF

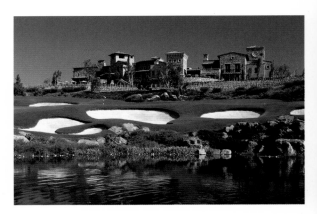

CONTENTS

PEBBLE BEACH GOLF LINKS

"The Greatest Meeting of land and Water in the World"...   *Robert Louis Stevenson*

When Samuel F.B. Morse first saw Pebble Beach, he knew he had discovered a special place. The grand-nephew of the inventor of the telegraph, Morse was the captain of Yale's 1906 undefeated football team. While in college he became friends with Templeton Crocker. That name was one of the Big Four – Crocker, Stanford, Huntington and Hopkins — who had built a railroad empire. Charles Crocker constructed Hotel Del Monte, a fashionable resort for the wealthy in 1879, and then constructed a railroad for access from San Francisco. The hotel had deteriorated and the railroad had been sold when Crocker decided to sell the land. Morse had worked for the Crocker Corporation for five years when, at the age of 30, he was chosen to go to the Monterey Peninsula to liquidate the assets. When Morse arrived, he was overwhelmed by the beauty. Four years later, in 1919, Morse formed a company that became Del Monte Properties and purchased some 7,000 acres that the Big Four had bought in 1879 for $35,000, or $5 an acre. Morse and his company paid $1.3 million, a princely sum at the time.

Above: The 18th hole at Pebble Beach during the AT&T Pebble Beach Pro-Am.

Left: The *Lone Cypress* on 17 Mile Drive, synonymous with Pebble Beach, one of the most photographed landmarks in the world.

"If I had only one course to play for the rest of my life it would be Pebble Beach."

Jack Nicklaus

Above: The par 3, 106 yard 7th hole.

Following pages: The par 5, 543 yard 18th hole.

There already had been plans for a golf course and homes to be built at Pebble Beach but Morse decided on fewer homes and a magnificent golf course, hiring Jack Neville and Douglas Grant as designers. Neville had won five state Amateurs and Grant had just returned from six years in Scotland and England, where he had studied the latest types of bunkering and greens construction on their championship courses, important elements in building a course that has become a mecca in golf. And, unlike most other prestigious courses in America, Pebble Beach Golf Links is open to the public.

Pebble Beach opened in 1929 and H. Chandler Egan was hired to toughen up the course for the 1929 U.S. Amateur Championship. Some of his changes were dramatic. He rebunkered the short, par -3 seventh hole, *Postage Stamp*, making an already intriguing hole more demanding. The already difficult par-5, fourteenth hole was lengthened 100 yards. But, contrary to

popular belief, he did not change the 18th hole– on the ocean from tee to green and one of golf's most famous finishing holes– from a 379 yard par 4 to a 548 yard par 5.

Pebble Beach has hosted four U.S. Opens, including the 100th U.S. Open in 2000; a PGA Championship; a PGA Tour Championship, and four U.S. Amateurs. Bing Crosby brought his tournament for his celebrity friends from Rancho Santa Fe in Southern California to Pebble Beach in 1947.

The Crosby became the AT&T Pebble Beach National Pro-Am Tournament in 1985.

Jack Nicklaus won the U.S. Open in 1972, a U.S. Amateur and three Crosbys on the course. Tom Watson prevented Jack from winning another U.S. Open on the course in 1982 with his dramatic chip-in birdie on the 17th hole of the final round. On that same hole during a Crosby, Arnold Palmer hit it long and over the cliff. He went down to the rocks below,

found his ball and, instead of taking a one-shot penalty and relief, whacked away until he wound up with a 12. That night at the watering hole, area bartenders were serving a drink they named "Palmer on the rocks."

The course record is 10-under-par 62 shared by Tom Kite (1983 Crosby) and by David Duval (1997 AT&T). Tiger Woods tied Jack Nicklaus for the all time U.S. Open record while winning the 100th U.S. Open in 2000 with a 12-under par at Pebble Beach.

THE BRIDGES
AT RANCHO SANTA FE

A Tuscan Masterpiece in the Coastal Foothills of San Diego's North County....

An exclusive, gated residential enclave nestled within the coastal foothills of one of California's most charming towns, The Bridges at Rancho Santa Fe exudes the breathtaking natural beauty of ancient Tuscany. Growing visibly as you approach the property, the magnificent 35,000 square foot clubhouse and 10,000 square foot Sports Centre create a dream-like vision, a centuries-old Italian country village transported in its entirety– stone-by-stone and complete with a landscape that includes olive trees, vineyards and citrus groves– from the countryside near Siena or Livorno to the hills of Rancho Santa Fe. Standing on the terrace of the stone clubhouse the sunshine and sea breezes complete the illusion as these environments, worlds apart, share much in common.

Above:The 35,000 square foot clubhouse glows in the afternoon sun in this view from the green of the par 4, 375 yard, 10th hole.

Right:The well-bunkered par 4, 434 yard, 18th hole is protected at the front by a pristine lake with an impressive display of aquatic plants.

"I found real joy at Rancho Santa Fe. Every environment there calls for simplicity and beauty - the gorgeous natural landscapes, the gentle topography, the nearby mountains."

Architect Lilian Rice, 1889-1938

When the creators of The Bridges first visited the site they were struck by its extraordinary beauty and remarkable similarity to the stunning landscapes of northern Tuscany – the gently rolling hillsides, rugged rock outcroppings and winding streams. They determined that an exceptional private residential community could preserve the beauty of the place and, with great care and planning, actually enhance it.

The architecture of the community's landmark buildings was designed to reflect timeless designs of old-world rural villages. Natural land formations and native vegetation were respected and spectacular bridges to traverse deep canyons were constructed to preserve the ruggedness of the site.

Left: A view across the green on the par 5, 571 yard 9th hole to the vineyards and clubhouse.

Above: The clubhouse terrace looks down on the signature 10th hole. From this vantage an ever changing show of color, texture and light unfolds.

Rancho Santa Fe is known for its equestrian trails, picturesque lanes and sprawling country estates. One of California's earliest planned communities, Rancho Santa Fe traces its history back to land grants from the Mexican government in the early 1800s. Renowned architect Lilian Rice designed the Rancho Santa Fe civic center, as well as many of its public buildings and private residences, in the Spanish Colonial Revival style.

A Protective Covenant was created in 1928 to preserve the Rancho Santa Fe lifestyle, which is more private and prestigious than its famous ocean-front neighbors, and in 1989, Rancho Santa Fe was designated a California State Historic Landmark.

San Diego's legendary near perfect year-round climate sets the stage for one of California's finest golf courses. The dramatic terrain of the 18-hole, par-71, course is unmatched in any

other in Southern California. Arching fairways, canyon carries and imposing bunkers and water hazards result in a course that is visually stimulating and challenging. Unique stress-ribbon bridges add character to the course and provide the essential links across deep canyons and waterways on the 10th and 11th holes. These bridges, nearly 300 feet long, are two of only three such bridges in the country.

The spectacular vistas from nearly every vantage point on the property,

of the rolling foothills and the deep canyon walls wandering through the course, add a sense of dimension to The Bridges that is found in few places around the world. The Bridges course was created to be a worthy adversary to the most accomplished golfers. It will entice you to hit great shots to reap rewards but will also extract a price for poor ones. The natural beauty of the site guarantees all who play will be sure to enjoy the experience.

Left: A series of waterfalls cascades from the 9th hole to the 18th under the stone bridge leading to the clubhouse.

Below: The par 4, 429 yard, 5th hole is guarded on the right by a series of bunkers and a lake that separates the 5th and 6th holes.

The clubhouse offers 360-degree views of the golf course, lakes, creeks, hillsides and bridges and is notable for the intimacy and charm of its many elegant rooms and galleries, striking in their perfect scale, rich finishes and fine antiques.

In addition to the formal dining room, the clubhouse includes a club grill with indoor and outdoor seating, a living room and an upstairs wine loft with a handsome private dining room. Men's and women's lounges and card rooms occupy opposite ends of the clubhouse, as do the separate locker rooms, steam rooms and spas. A large, fully stocked pro shop overlooks the 18th green.

The 10,000 square foot Sports Centre provides the finest health and fitness facilities, including the most current cardio and weight training equipment, and a hardwood floor gym. Separate men's and women's lounges include lockers, saunas, massage rooms and spas. Another spa is outdoors, near the lap pool and wading pool.

The Bridges offers a limited number of homes, homesites and villas amidst the hillsides, fairways and orchards of this secluded private community.

Above and right: The 35,000 square foot clubhouse is the center of community activities.

Far right: The stress-ribbon bridge leading to the green of the par 3, 165 yard, 11th hole.

ROARING FORK CLUB

Rustic Log Cabins, a Jack Nicklaus Signature Course, World-Class Fly Fishing and the Heritage of Colorado's Rocky Mountains....

The Roaring Fork Club encompasses 282 acres along the banks of the Roaring Fork River– legendary to the world's fly fishermen– between Basalt and Aspen, Colorado. Just down the valley The Frying Pan awaits, a pilgrimage for the avid sportsman in its own right. Factor in a championship Jack Nicklaus Signature Course and a limited number of well-crafted log cabins and suites accessible only by golf carts, and the result is a truly unforgettable experience. The Club's developers created a golf and fishing experience that is true to the timeless traditions of each sport in an environment that focuses heavily on family traditions, neighborly interaction and communion with nature. World-class fishing and Jack Nicklaus golf– it's almost too good to be true and when you add some of Colorado's most spectacular terrain to the mix it can prove to be an intoxicating combination.

Left: From the tees, across the Roaring Fork River, to the par 4, 366 yard 6th hole in the fall. The Roaring Fork River is known for some of the world's best trout fishing.

Above: Spring Creek protects the front of the 6th hole on the Jack Nicklaus Signature Course at the Roaring Fork Club. Spring Creek was carefully crafted by the developers and is meticulously managed including stocking with impressive brown and rainbow trout.

"Mother Nature gave us an amphitheater with rugged mountains, stone benches and a beautiful winding river. I've rarely seen a site so naturally suited for a signature golf course."

Jack Nicklaus

The 18 hole Nicklaus course design was inspired by the stone outcroppings, tall stands of cottonwoods and rolling meadows that highlight the landscape. The course has five holes that play on or near the fast moving waters of the Roaring Fork River or Spring Creek, while the first five holes

The Club's 6,600 foot elevation, opposed to higher altitude courses near Aspen and Snowmass, allows members a longer playing season. Spring days are idyllic; summer is slow and easy, and fall days bring a riot of color to the landscape.

The signature 16th hole is a par 3 with the Roaring Fork River

play through pristine wetlands and crystal clear lakes teeming with trout, some that are monsters.

The par-72 course plays 7,130 yards from the Black tees creating a true test for low handicappers and as short as 5,255 yards from the Rose tees for those desiring an equal challenge. The course features a near perfect east-west orientation allowing for dramatic morning and afternoon sun and stunning mountain views.

guarding the right side from tee to green, Spring Creek protects the left and the entire flight of the ball as the shot makes its way to a sloping green that is over wetlands.

The Club offers a cutting-edge golf school for members looking to improve their game. The golf professional team is a group of the country's leading researchers in golf and sports science. The team's teaching components are tailor-made to meet individual

Above: A large lake and strategically place bunkers await the errant tee shot on the dogleg left, par 4, 399 yard 11th hole.

Right: Canadian geese, *Bránta canadénsis*, enjoy the tranquility of a summer afternoon in Spring Creek, which guards the left side of the par 3, 177 yard 16th hole seen here from the Rose tees.

golfer's specific needs and gives the tools needed to improve their game on every level. Strong emphasis is placed on video analysis, swing plane evaluation, mental conditioning, shot preparation and physical exercise. The club also offers a full service golf shop, caddie programs, 11,700 sq.ft. of practice greens and PGA instructors.

Left: A fly fisherman works the riffles in Spring Creek in front of a rustic streamside cabin.

Far left: The 15th hole is bordered by Spring Creek on the right and towering Cottonwoods to the left.

Fishing the Roaring Fork Club is an angler's paradise with a plethora of pristine fishing venues from which to choose. The Club features 1.5 miles of Gold Medal waters along the internationally

acclaimed Roaring Fork River, the mile long, 20 foot wide, spring-fed Spring Creek, eight stocked trout ponds and the nearby Frying Pan River. Experts and beginners alike

will find a place to hone their intuition and skills and test their mettle against brook, brown and rainbow trout.

A variety of fly fishing work-shops and guided experiences for all ages and abilities are offered to members. Fishing aficionados

may choose to take guided trips down the Roaring Fork or Frying Pan rivers in one of the club's drift boats or sign up for one of many workshops, led by the Roaring Fork Club's professional fishing staff, held on the club's grounds.

Architecture of the Club's cabins and suites is a rustic yet elegant blend of hand-hewn log cabins and suites that are reminiscent of the civilized traditions of the "great camps" of the Adirondacks.

The Roaring Fork Club is not an exclusive housing development built around a golf course, it is a

private family sporting club and membership is available on an invitation-only basis and is limited. Club members may own one of the Roaring Fork Club's 48 cabins individually or as a part of the Cabin Membership Program with a 1/4 or 1/6 deeded interest.

Left: The architecture of the Roaring Fork Club reflects the natural beauty of its surroundings and is reminiscent of the civilized traditions of the "great camps" of the Adirondacks.

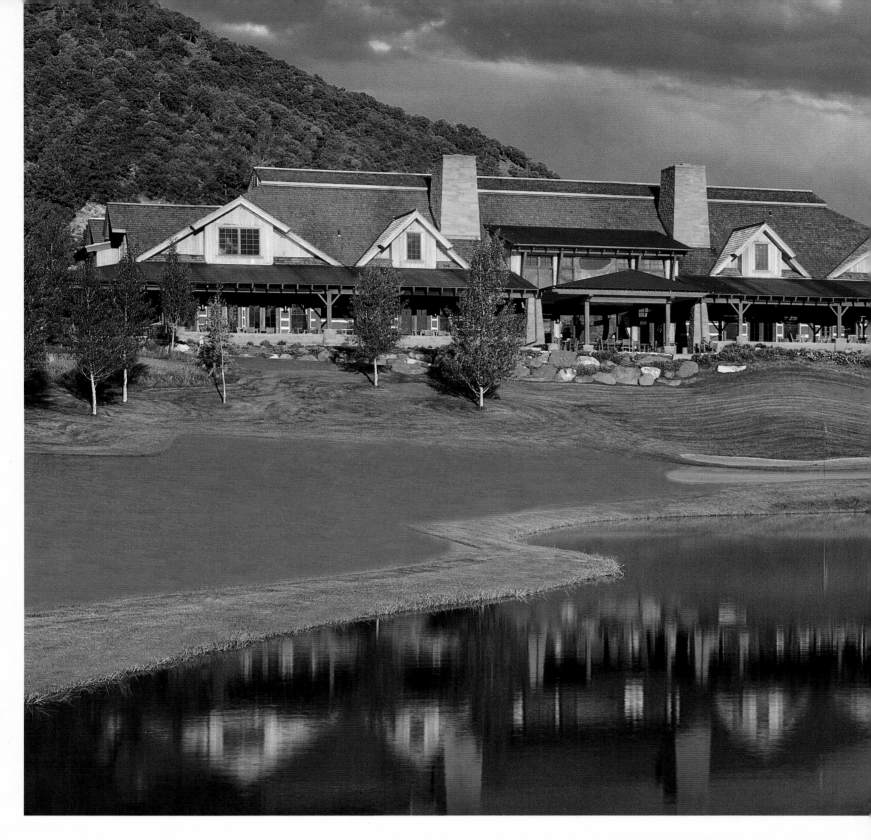

The Club's twelve Member Suites are available on a 1/6 ownership basis. Located directly across from the Members' Lodge, the Club's suites offer dramatic views of the front nine, valley and mountains and are near the swimming pool and tennis courts.

The Member Suites' wood floors, richly appointed furnishings and two fireplaces– one indoors and the other outdoors on the wrap around patio– capture the warmth and luxury of the club. Suite owners are entitled to use the Suites sixty days or more per year, with the privilege to use multiple Suites simultaneously on a space available basis.

The Member's Lodge, with a chinked timber exterior, warm inviting interior and expansive views is the heart of the Roaring Fork Club. Reminiscent of the great National Park lodges, the Members' Lodge has a solidly elegant appeal and sense of timeless

Right: The living room of one of the Club's twelve Member Suites.

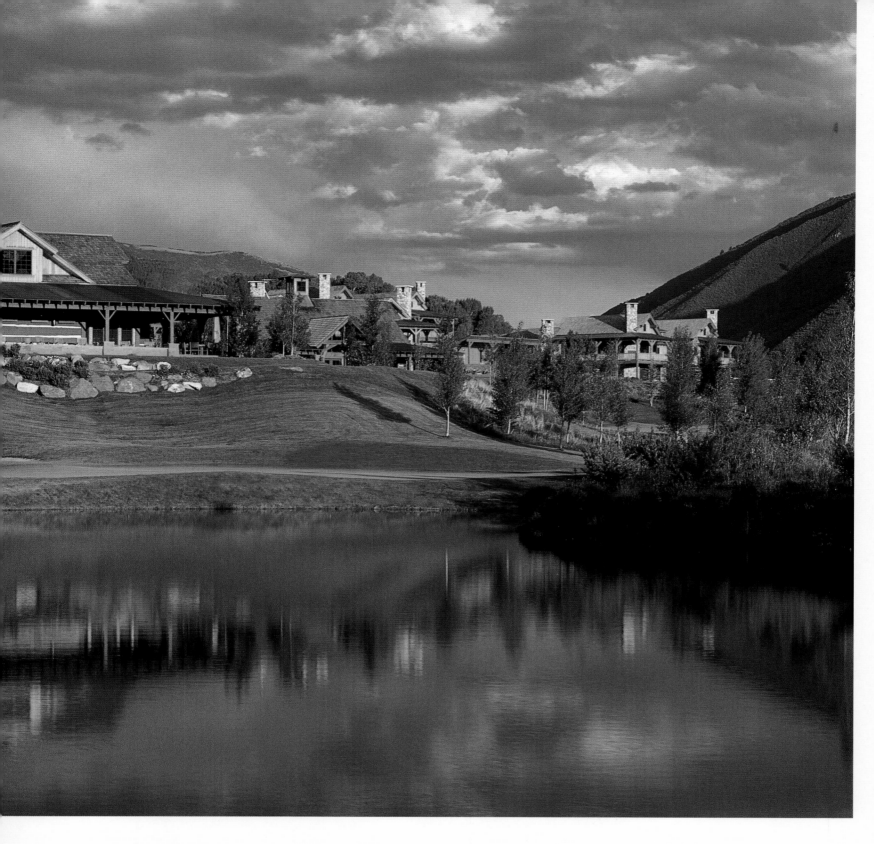

style that harkens memories of days gone by. The comfortable 2-story

Great Room, with its moss rock fireplace, and the veranda overlooking the 18th hole are places to gather and reflect on the day's adventures. The lodge also houses a library with billiards, vintner room, fitness and business facilities, as well as men's and women's locker rooms.

The Roaring Fork Club winter season is a time

of beauty and excitement with Aspen and Snowmass ski resorts, just 15 miles away, offering the finest winter activities, nightlife and shopping.

The Roaring Fork Club was conceived and developed by Jim Light, Jim Chaffin and David Wilhelm, three of the most distinguished and highly principled developers in the business.

Above: The Members Lodge overlooking the par 4, 422 yard 18th hole at sunset.

Left: A cozy evening in the Great Room of one of the Club's 48 Log Cabins.

FOUR SEASONS RESORT AVIARA GOLF CLUB

A Sanctuary at the Water's Edge....

I n the still of the morning, as a warm sun dries the dewy grass, you can hear the birds take flight over Batiquitos Lagoon. The morning hush is broken by the flap of wings, as earth and sky meet in a giant rush of great blue herons, terns and kestrels, lifting off from their watery sanctuary, circling the lush gardens of the golf course, then settling once more beside the salt-water lagoon. This is nature as it was meant to be... this is Four Seasons Resort Aviara.

Named for its intimate yet respectful relationship with nature, Aviara is a creative blend of terms... *aviary*, a home for birds, and *terra*, the earth. Aviara's golf course was created from the inspired design of golf legend Arnold Palmer, and was meticulously sculpted from the area's native chaparral. Blankets of wildflowers in a colorful palette reach out to the very edge of fairways and greens. Coastal sage rolls thickly across surrounding hillsides and bubbling streams of sparkling water spill alongside many of the holes.

Right: The back side of the island green on the par 3, 201 yard 3rd hole.

Above: The 32.000 square foot clubhouse behind the green on the par 4, 443 yard 18th hole at the Four Seasons Aviara Golf Club.

Named for its intimate yet respectful relationship with nature, Aviara is a creative blend of terms... aviary, a home for birds, and terra, the earth...

It took nearly a decade to complete Aviara Golf Club, so sensitive were its builders to the delicate ecological balance between man and nature. Ultimate care was taken to preserve the vitally important wetlands adjacent to the site... now, the 180 acres of the golf course are merely a beautiful extension of nature's own handiwork, that keeps drawing wildlife to the area. Play is relaxed with few parallel fairways.

At Aviara, Arnold Palmer has created intricate shotmaking challenges along the entire 7,007 yards of the championship layout. Water hazards in the form of streams and waterfalls are

with breathtaking views of Batiquitos Lagoon and the Pacific Ocean beyond. An occasional coyote or bobcat might be glimpsed at the first light of day or as dusk settles in for the evening. Red-tailed hawks are a frequent sight as they circle the golf course, soaring gracefully on gentle updrafts.

Following the natural topography of three gentle valleys, the golf course at Aviara is a links-style layout designed to challenge golfers of every ability. Hillside tees play down to landing areas in the valleys; with gentle hills rising on all sides, players feel the same sense of solitude and tranquillity

positioned visually as natural extensions of the lagoon. Eucalyptus trees, wildflowers and sagebrush line the fairways, subtly increasing the golfer's level of skill. At the same time, the expansive fairways and greens offer forgiving landing areas, as well as uninterrupted views. Hole by hole, golfers will discover why both *Golf Digest* and *Golf Magazine* have named Aviara one of the best resort courses in the country.

Aviara's clubhouse facilities are as thoughtfully presented as the course itself. With understated elegance, the two-story clubhouse in the Spanish

Above: The practice putting green in front of the award-winning 32,000 square foot clubhouse designed in early California's Spanish Colonial architectural style.

Above: A side view of the par 5, 536 yard 8th green with water along the fairway to the left and completely protecting the green in front.

Left: The 11th hole, par 3, 189 yards, is all carry with water in front of the green and stream on the right.

Colonial style houses men's and women's locker facilities, a complete golf shop, and the Argyle restaurant and lounge, both of which provide the perfect setting for relaxing and taking in the views. Aviara's state-of-the-art digital video systems in the learning center and on the practice tee are equipped with audio voice over systems, so your individual instruction is not lost or forgotten. This way, your take-home video tape will enable you to keep improving long after your 2 or 3 day instruction program has ended, because you will be able to

"re-take" your instruction at home as often as you like. If questions come up later, you're only a toll-free call away from your instructor.

As you step onto the incomparable course at Aviara Golf Club, you step into a world of timeless natural beauty. This is a magical place of wildlife and water, chaparral and flowers, and the ever challenging lure of golf. This is what the game was meant to be... this is Four Seasons Resort Aviara.

Above: The library in the two-story clubhouse provides the perfect place for relaxing and gathering with friends.

Right: The backside view of the green on the par 3, 201 yard 14th hole looking west toward the tees.

SILVERLEAF

The Embodiment of Sonoran Desert Elegance in Scottsdale's McDowell Mountains...

S eemingly etched into the heart of the Sonoran Desert in Scottsdale, Arizona, Silverleaf is an exclusive enclave destined to rank among the finest communities in the world. Throughout this undisturbed realm of High Sonoran Desert, one senses the grandeur of life and the rhythm of the desert as giant saguaros stand like silent sentinels patiently observing the passage of time. Far above the city lights below, one may pause to watch a lingering sunset and feel the gentle evening breeze with its subtle hint of sage.

At the center of this prestigious community, the new Tom Weiskopf-designed Silverleaf course has been sculpted from the land with great care and concern for the delicate desert environment. Surely one of the crowning achievements in Weiskopf's illustrious career, the 7,267-yard course winds unobtrusively through the pristine desert, its meticulously maintained tees, fairways and greens stand in contrast with the rich desert palette of saguaro, ocotillo, sage and palo verde.

Above: A view from the back side of the green of the par 4, 466-yard 18th hole. The green is protected to the left by a massive bunker system.

Left: The par 4, 423-yard 6th hole is best played from the right-hand side of the fairway approaching the green, which is guarded at the left and back by large, deep hand-raked sand bunkers.

Elements of the Silverleaf course have been carefully positioned to capture dramatic vistas of the valley below, the McDowell Mountain peaks and passes above and the tranquil essence of the Sonoran Desert. Multiple tee placements, ranging from 5,199-yards at the forward tees to 7,267-yards at the championship tees, assure a challenge appropriate for golfers at all levels of play. The real challenge here may be to avoid being captivated by the natural charms of the surrounding terrain.

Silverleaf will be a community of remarkable beauty– its amenities and desert landscape nestled within North Scottsdale's McDowell Mountains. The community will have

three distinct neighborhoods: The Parks, Upper Canyon and Horseshoe Canyon.

The Parks will feature intimate parkside homes ranging from 2,600 to more than 5,000 sq. ft. as well as custom homes in an area bordering the 2nd, 3rd, 8th, 9th and 10th holes and featuring natural desert washes, conservation areas and 7 parks.

The Upper Canyon offers large estate homesites that range in size from 1.1 acres to more than 30 acres. Perched high above the Valley floor overlooking the 6th, 7th and 8th holes of the Silverleaf course, these spectacular homesites offer breathtaking views of city lights and golf course vistas.

Horseshoe Canyon occupies an unparalled example of the High Sonoran Desert.

Clockwise from above left: The par 3, 234-yard 16th hole at sunset. Above right: An aerial view from the back right of the par 3, 217-yard 7th hole. Above: The par 4, 388-yard 11th hole at sunrise.

Left: *Tom's Thumb* is visible on the peak behind the par 5, 576-yard 14th hole.

All Silverleaf homesites have been carefully planned to allow a wide range of architectural expressions, and every property is situated to emphasize privacy. Each home will suit the individual tastes of the owner with design parameters that will ensure harmony with the desert landscape, creating a unique desert community. Silverleaf will be a unique desert community distinguished by its individuality.

Silverleaf's clubhouse, constructed with native materials and showcasing a rural Mediterranean flair, will feature gathering places intimate enough for two yet expansive enough for festive gatherings. A spa with indoor-outdoor massage suites and a full range of services will offer an opportunity to reflect and rejuvenate. At night, Silverleaf will shine. Desert plants, wildlife, stars and moonlight will lend an air of mystery and enchantment while the restaurant will offer superb cuisine, fine wines and soft ambience in a captivating setting.

Silverleaf draws upon the considerable experience, resources and talents of DMB Associates, Inc. DMB's name is synonymous with high-quality large-scale real estate developments with projects that include the award-winning DC Ranch residential community; Lahontan, a private golf community in North Lake Tahoe; Forest Highlands, an 1,100-acre private community with two Tom Weiskopf courses in the mountains of Flagstaff, Arizona, and Santaluz, a 3,800-acre private golf community with a Rees Jones course in Rancho Santa Fe, California.

Above: A saguaro stands as a silent sentinel along the back side of the green on the par 5, 544-yard 3rd hole.

Above right: The par 3, 217-yard, 7th hole from the tees.

Right: An azure lake protects the right side of the par 4, 395-yard, 13th hole and awaits the overzealous approach shot.

THE HIGHLANDS
AT BRECKENRIDGE

Jack Nicklaus Designed Golf in the Colorado High Country...

The oldest continuously occupied mountain town in Colorado, Breckenridge traces its roots back through more than 150 years to the Colorado gold rush and its Victorian beginnings, a time that found the town awash with the hopes and dreams of miners seeking fortunes in gold and merchants eager to supply food, beverage and all matters of comfort and merchandise. Today, the Town of Breckenridge still clings to its Victorian architecture and enjoys status earned as a National Historic District with a sense of community that is at the forefront of all activity and unparalleled in any other American resort town. Here, the quality of life is an important part of every decision, and the only development projects that are allowed to proceed are those that better the community.

Above: The Highlands at Breckenridge, nestled in Colorado's Blue River Valley, offers incomparable outdoor recreational opportunities.

Right: Poppy fields on the par 3, 242 yard, 5th hole on the Elk course.

The Highlands at Breckenridge, an impressive master planned residential golf community encompassing approximately 1200 acres in Colorado's Blue River Valley, is true to the grand traditions of the game of golf, Breckenridge heritage, and the natural wonders of the Colorado high country. Pine, aspen and Engleman spruce blanket the hillsides while 27 holes of Nicklaus designed golf wind their way through pristine

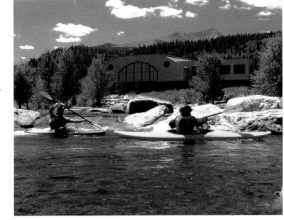

meadows and protected wetland areas. The wetland areas provide nature preserves within The Highlands that include a series of picturesque beaver ponds that lie along the fairways and greens of the Beaver course.

The Highlands at Breckenridge is the only golf course community within the Town of Breckenridge. In addition to the Jack Nicklaus signature golf course, The Highlands enjoys a close proximity to world-class skiing, views of the spectacular Ten Mile Range, and the shops and restaurants of Main Street. The Highlands dedicated 127 acres of the project, including 77 acres for an additional nine holes for

the golf course and 11 acres for the new Ralph M. Rounds Memorial Park, to the Town of Breckenridge. The park, named after one of the founders of Breckenridge Lands, Inc. and the Breckenridge Ski Area, includes lakeside fishing areas, fishing piers, hiking paths, boardwalks across wetlands and a grass play area.

Breckenridge Golf Club, with an elevation of 9324 feet, is owned and operated by the Town of Breckenridge and is all one would expect to find in a Jack Nicklaus signature course. The 27 hole layout consists of three nines offering a chance to play the course in three different configurations. The Bear course plays 3694

the green and shots that come in too low, or too long, present a tricky recovery shot. The 206 yard, 4th hole is a straight-away par 3 that gives a chance to calm the nerves or recover from a bad shot on the previous hole.

The 3563 yard Beaver course offers a unique golfing experience as the course works its way along a series of beaver ponds that at times may spill onto the cart paths. These nine holes lie in a riparian biotic community that is so rich in the flora and fauna of the Blue River Valley that at times you may find yourself surprised anyone would be allowed to even hike in the area, much less drive a cart through it.

yards through meadowlands with water coming into play on the 1st, 3rd, 7th and 8th holes. The par 4, 403 yard, 3rd hole has a lake that guards the front of a very shallow green and most of the right side of the fairway. Shots too short are in the lake or in the bunker at the left front of

It is a credit to the careful management of the course that the Beaver course is in existence. Here, if you can keep your mind on the game, the par 3, 177 yard 3rd hole and the par 4, 405 yard 6th hole offer realistic birdie

Top left: Kayaks test the rapids on the reconstructed Blue River at the Breckenridge Recreation Center. The river, destroyed by dredging in the late 1800s, has been carefully restored by the Town of Breckenridge.

Left: A fly fisherman enjoys the waters of the fishing lake in Ralph M. Rounds Memorial Park. The Highlands dedicated the park to the Town of Breckenridge for community use.

Above: The par 4, 435 yard 7th hole on the Elk course is a downhill dogleg right offering spectacular views of the valley below.

Below: The expansive vista from The Highlands and the 403 yard, par 4 3rd hole of the Bear course. The lake and bunker in the front penalize any short shots. Shots coming into the green low will end up long and present a tricky recovery shot.

opportunities while the extremely narrow par 4, 409 yard, 7th hole, with its two-tiered green, and the 580 yard, par 5, 8th hole, with streams and beaver ponds everywhere, can pose back-to-back problems for the unlucky or the unwary. The approach shot on the 8th hole must clear the beaver ponds to find the green.

The Elk course is the newest addition to Breckenridge Golf Club, opening in the summer of 2001. This nine hole, 3563 yard, layout plays up and down hillsides of The Highlands offering spectacular vistas of the valley below and the mountains in the distance. The 242 yard, par 3, 5th hole is surely one of the most colorful golf holes we've ever seen, playing over a field of poppys stretching from tee to green. The 281 yard, par 4, 6th hole is a short par 4 that offers an excellent chance for a birdie, as is

the 385 yard, par 4, 1st hole which is wide open, but guarded on the right by a large sand bunker and a lake. The 8th hole, a 576 yard par five, is well-bunkered with fairway bunkers in front of the green and bunkers to the left, right and rear. All in all, this is an easy hole to lose a stroke or two, as is the 2nd hole, another par 5, that plays to 574 yards from the gold tees with tee shots across water to a very narrow fairway.

Maintenance at Breckenridge Golf Club ranks among the best mountain courses and the PGA professional staff

exhibits a level of quality and service that is normally found only in the finest private clubs.

The Highlands at Breckenridge Sets a New Benchmark for Sensitive Community Design...

Years of thought and careful planning have preceded the development of The Highlands. The project, designed to exist in harmony with its dramatic mountain setting, utilizes the "building envelope" method of determining a suitable area for building on each parcel to best preserve the community's natural environment and mountain views.

Land Use Restrictions and Design Guidelines of The Highlands provide for strict supervision of architectural style, exterior colors and materials, building heights and other elements of construction. They also provide for a Review Board to review and approve plans for homes within the community.

The Highlands at Breckenridge is a partnership between Lincoln North, Inc. and Highlands Management Group, Inc. The principals of Lincoln North are members of the Rounds family, the original developer of the Breckenridge Ski area, that has owned the property for more than 35 years. They are also developers of West Ridge and Shock Hill. The principals of Highlands Management Group are residential land developers well-known for developing successful

communities including Singletree near Vail, Colorado; Desert Highlands in Scottsdale, Arizona; Forest Highlands near Flagstaff, Arizona; Mira Vista in Fort Worth, Texas, and Lahontan near Lake Tahoe, California.

Top left: The Ten Mile Range in winter. Breckenridge receives an average of 300 inches of snow a year and was the most visited ski resort in North America for two of the last three years.

Above: The Williams home, designed by Hagman Architects of Aspen, is landscaped with English gardens spread among the native pine.

Left: The par 5, 580 yard 8th hole on the Beaver course. You must clear the beaver ponds in front of the green on your approach shot.

PELICAN HILL
GOLF CLUB

Gracious Style in the Old California Tradition at Newport Coast....

A long a pristine stretch of the Pacific shoreline, just off the famed Pacific Coast Highway, lies the stately California mission-style Pelican Hill Golf Club, home to one of Southern California's most memorable golfing experiences. Born of a desire to maintain the area's natural essence, Pelican Hill is a stunning example of craftsmanship combined with an uncompromised respect for the land. Thirty-six holes of golf sit atop some of the finest oceanfront acreage in all of California, barely creating a disturbance, but rather enhancing the already significant beauty of the coastline.

A great legacy comes with this land, where cattle once roamed the rolling hillsides and rugged coastal canyons of the old Irvine Ranch. Today, golfers enjoy the panoramic views that sweep from Newport Harbor west to Catalina Island and south to Laguna Beach. Located within the prestigious resort community of Newport Coast, Pelican Hill Golf Club preserves the coastal lands and creates a memorable golf challenge.

Above: Pelican Hill's Santa Barbara Mission-style golf clubhouse and golf shop.

Left: *Double Trouble,* the par 3, 123 yard 13th hole on the Ocean South Course.

"The first ten years have been richly rewarding, and like most golf clubs, Pelican Hill continues to mature with age... there are exciting things in store for Pelican Hill."

Tom Fazio, Architect

Award-winning course architect Tom Fazio created two distinct 18-hole layouts at Pelican Hill– the Ocean North and the Ocean South courses. First to debut in 1991 was the Ocean South Course, a skillful combination of wandering canyons, eucalyptus groves and pine forests suddenly traversing to open fairways gently rolling terrain, with dramatic canyon-crossing shots, breathtaking views and a spectacular series of holes built right along the coastline. *Golf Digest* named Pelican Hill's Ocean South Course as the *Best New Resort Course* of 1992 in January of 1993, the first in a continuing series of accolades and honors.

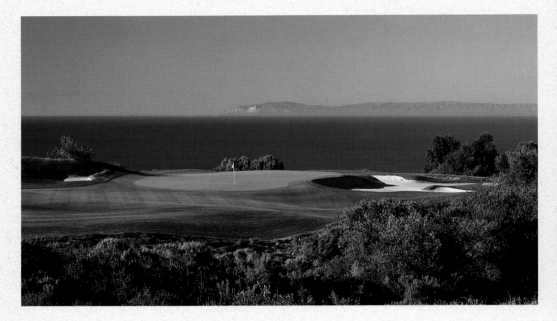

along dramatic seaside cliffs. Fazio describes the Ocean South Course as "... a game of contrast and versatility... golf at its most exhilarating!"

From high above the Pacific Ocean, the Ocean South Course descends to bermuda fairways lined by towering eucalyptus, blooming coral and pine trees. Challenging Penncross bent grass greens, framed by white sand bunkers, combine with magnificent ocean vistas providing an inspiring experience.

Built across the face of Pelican Hill, the Ocean South Course features a

The 12th hole, *Pelican's Nest*, is a 212 yard par 3 that often plays into the ocean breeze and the 13th hole, *Double Trouble*, is a 121 yard par 3 surrounded by sculpted sand bunkers, are two of golf's most beautiful and more difficult holes. Carved from the rugged rock outcroppings of Pelican Point, these par 3s hug the bluffs and offer dramatic views of Pacific surf on the beach below.

Double Cross, the 442 yard, par 4, 18th hole and *On the Rocks*, the 195 yard, par 3, 7th hole are two more of 18 reasons the Ocean South Course has become a California tradition.

Above: 16th hole, *Lone Tree*, 220 yard, par 3, Ocean South Course.

Right: 18th hole, *Double Cross*, 442 yard, par 4, Ocean South Course.

azio's second layout at Pelican Hill, the Ocean North Course, opened in 1993 and soon received accolades similar to those bestowed on the earlier Ocean South Course, including its rating by *Golf Magazine* as one of the *Top 10 New Resort Courses for 1993.* Fashioned in the Scottish links tradition, this Fazio design meanders back and forth along an elevated plateau situated high above the deep-blue Pacific. On the distant ocean, crisp white sails snap in the breeze as yachts cruise the waters offshore.

features rolling, links-like terrain that promotes creative shotmaking. Like the Ocean South course, the Ocean

playing field for players of different abilities, challenging low handicap golfers, but still providing enjoyable rounds for the higher handicap players.

Pelican's Ocean North Course encompasses elevation changes of 100 to 300 feet, creating a landscape with uninterrupted ocean views as well as an abundance of different shot values. The natural California coastal vegetation grows in the canyons and on

Built along a series of coastal plateaus and canyons, the Ocean North Course

North course has five different sets of tees designed to provide a level

the hillsides, stopping just short of fairways and greens. The famed 17th

hole, a 545 yard par 5 aptly named *Gut Check*, is played from an elevated canyon and the green is heavily bunkered along the right side, most

Far left: The 2nd hole on the Ocean North Course, *Postage Stamp*, a 189 yard par 3, at sunset.

Left: *Double Down*, the 426 yard, par 4, 18th hole on the Ocean North Course from behind the green.

Below: A panoramic view of the clubhouse, 1st tee and 18th fairway.

tee to a narrow fairway. There is a long uphill carry across a lake and a definitely not for the faint of heart or weak-kneed.

After a satisfying day on the golf course, players can retire to the richly appointed comfort of Pelican Hill's gracious Santa Barbara mission-style clubhouse, reminiscent of the mood and elegance of old California. All the amenities of the finest private country club are available to the general public, from drive-up valet service to the eager assistance of trained golf professionals. The elegant Golf Shop at Pelican Hill, with its cozy fireplace and overstuffed chairs, offers the latest in equipment, attire,

gifts and accessories.

At the Glenn Deck Golf Academy at Pelican Hill, students receive the same quality of instruction that is typical of every aspect of the golf experience found at Pelican Hill Golf Club. A staff composed exclusively of PGA teaching professionals

combines personalized attention with state-of-the-art technology in

an effort to address each individual's natural level of ability.

From the coastal canyons to the seaside cliffs, Pelican Hill Golf Club epitomizes the graceful, old-world charm of Southern California at its finest, enhanced further by the significant beauty of the coastline.

Above: *Gut Check*, the 543 yard, par 5, 17th hole on the Ocean North Course.

Far left: *On the Rocks*, the 195 yard, par 3, 7th hole on the Ocean South Course.

Left: *Horizon*, the 415 yard, par 4, 14th hole on the Ocean North Course.

MARRIOTT'S
NEWPORT COAST® VILLAS

Classic Elegance Along the Pacific Ocean...

O verlooking the Pacific Ocean in Newport Coast, California, Marriott's Newport Coast Villas are an irresistible destination that surpasses all expectations. The 75 acre resort is bordered by championship golf, breathtaking views of the Pacific and the spectacular Crystal Cove State Park. The Resort and local areas offer virtually unlimited attractions and activities including golf, yachting, tennis, diving, fishing, wind surfing and surfing, and close proximity to several world-class theme parks and renowned shopping at South Coast Plaza and Fashion Island.

The Resort's on site amenities include three swimming pools, two tennis courts, beach access, barbecue grills and picnic areas, a state-of-the-art fitness center and Spa Pacifica for facials, sauna and massages. The MarketPlace is available for light meals. Vacation owners also enjoy the facilities at the nearby Newport Beach Marriott Hotel & Tennis Club. The renowned Pelican Hill Golf Club and its two Tom Fazio designed golf courses are adjacent to the resort.

Above: Marriott's Newport Coast® Villas courtyard with the ocean beyond.

Right: *Lone Tree*, the par 3, 216 yard 16th hole on the Ocean South Course at Pelican Hill Golf Club, Newport Coast, California.

The Newport Coast Villas offer a private oasis with unique resort amenities, elegant appointments and striking coastal views. Each of the 1,240-square foot two bedroom, two bathroom Villas can accommodate up to eight people. The luxurious master suite offers a king size bed, television, stretch and soak tub, and a separate bath with twin showerheads while the guestroom features a full bath, queen bed, double sleeper sofa and television. A spacious living area provides a queen sleeper sofa and an entertainment center. The Villa's dining area accommodates six with breakfast bar for two.

The Villa's deluxe kitchen is fully equipped with dishwasher, oven, microwave, full size refrigerator and dinnerware service for eight. Other Villa amenities include a private balcony or patio with table and chairs, utility room with a washer and dryer and linens for eight.

Located amidst the best of coastal Orange County, Marriott's Newport Coast® Villas is a hillside haven in and of itself. Marriott's Newport Coast® Villas and Vacation Club International offer several ownership options to fit one's travel needs. Additionally, Villas owners have access to the magnificent Pelican Hill Golf Club, a mecca for golf enthusiasts who travel from around the world to test their skills on the courses at Newport Coast. Pelican Hill's award-winning golf courses and club-house, highly acclaimed restaurant, men's and

women's locker facilities, golf shop and PGA professional teaching staff rank consistently among the best in the world.

Overlooking the sparkling Pacific, Marriott's Newport Coast® Villas are set in lush gardens and under towering palms, each offering the spaciousness and comfort of a private residence.

Top left: The courtyard fountains at dusk.

Top right: One of the Villa's three pools.

Above: Architectural detail of the Villas with Santa Catalina Island in the distance.

Left: The Villas and the Newport Beach coastline.

MARRIOTT'S DESERT SPRINGS
THE ULTIMATE CALIFORNIA DESERT RETREAT

In a magical setting of date palms, snow-dusted mountain peaks and warm, caressing sunshine awaits a desert resort unlike any other... Marriott's Desert Springs Resort & Spa.

From the moment you enter the grounds, crossing the palm tree-lined boulevard, passing lakes and lagoons sparkling in the sunlight, you realize this will be an experience to be savored. Everywhere, perfectly manicured grounds delight the senses.

Surrounded by thirty-six holes of championship golf verdantly spread along the floor of Southern California's Coachella Valley, Marriott's Desert Springs Resort & Spa is a tropical desert oasis offering life's finest pleasures. Flamingos, swans and tropical birds grace acres of lushly planted English gardens, meandering waterways and tranquil lagoons.

Arriving at the resort, with its massive atrium lobby complete with cascading waterfalls and an indoor lake, guests can board a gondola-style boat for a relaxing cruise along the property's wandering canals.

The resort's luxurious guestrooms and well appointed suites are surrounded by swimming pools, tennis courts, two golf courses and the distinctive Spa at Desert Springs, which encompasses 30,000 square-feet of fitness and body therapy facilities. For pure pleasure, nothing surpasses the rejuvenating qualities of a languid day at the Spa. Therapeutic thermal baths, herbal wraps and mud body masques refresh the mind and soothe the soul. Guests from around the world travel to Marriott's Desert Springs for its facial and body treatments, many of which draw from the natural healing elements of the desert.

Above: The resort boulevard and the elevated 16th tee.

Right: The 3rd Green to the 15th Green on the Palm Course.

Marriott's Desert Springs Offers Unparalleled Beauty and Unlimited Recreational Possibilities...

Wrapped around the perimeter of the hotel are two Ted Robinson designed championship golf courses. Both the Palms Course and the Valley course are truly visual feasts. Each features an abundance of the magnificent waterfalls, pristine lakes and sparkling streams, flowers and palms for which this award-winning architect, is known. A day on either the Palms Course or the Valley Course is both an adventure and a shot making challenge.

Ted Robinson's designs incorporate more than thirty-five acres of lagoons, streams and waterfalls that criss-cross Marriott's Desert Springs Resort & Spa, creating a memorable series of hazards and rewards. On the Palms Course nine of the eighteen holes have water coming into play. The seventeenth hole is a 160 yard par 3 with an island green. The Valley Course offers eight holes with water features including another island green on the 316 yard, par 4, sixteenth hole. The sixth hole on the Valley Course features a 222 yard par 3 with water on both sides to the green. Anything short, left or right of the green, is sure to be wet.

More than a million cubic yards of desert sand were molded and shaped into the hills and valleys that create the Palms Course and the Valley Course. Both offer multiple tee boxes, strategic bunkering and split-level or island greens. Players of the Valley Course and Palms Course are treated to imposing views of the rugged San Jacinto Mountains and Santa Rosa Mountains as they rise dramatically from the desert floor.

The par 5, 528 yard, first hole on the Palms Course with an afternoon view across the Palm Desert Valley to the Santa Rosa Mountains.

Each of the 36 holes that comprise the Marriott's Desert Springs golf experience offers a unique challenge. The Palms Course features gently rolling terrain, lots of water, and close-up views of the sprawling resort. On the Valley Course, the eighteenth hole is considered by many to be the best finishing hole in the Coachella Valley. A semi-elevated tee box transitions to a two-tiered fairway, guarded by bunkers on both sides. To finish this 403 yard, par 4, players must hit over water to the three-tiered green, guarded in front by a lake and a beautiful, but challenging, series of waterfalls.

Far left: The Spa at Marriott's Desert Springs is a full-service European health spa with its own private pool.

Left: Chilean Flamingos congregate in a lagoon in front of the 16th tee on the 6,761 yard Palms Course.

Below: The par 3, 162 yard, third hole is all carry and a part of the resort's entry experience.

The Seventeenth hole on the Palms Course is one of the more photogenic holes at the resort. The green of this remarkable par 3 is surrounded by water on all sides and is accessible only by footbridge. The fun begins when the successful golfer carries the ball directly over cascading waterfalls onto the island, nearly 160 yards from the tee.

For days that are just too busy for a full round of golf, or to hone your putting skills before or after a round, Ted Robinson designed The Greens, America's first 18-hole putting course, a concept since immolated by a host of others.

A visit to Marriott's Desert Springs Resort & Spa is refreshment for the spirit and an adventure for the soul, in the heart of thriving Palm Desert. Its scenic splendor and impeccable service will leave you longing to return to this desert oasis.

Right: Waterfalls guard the green of the par 3, 160 yard, 17th hole on the Palms Course.

Below: Snow covers Mt. San Jacinto behind the eighteenth tee on the Palms Course.

Top: The green on the dogleg left, par 4, 423 yard eighteenth hole on the Palms Course, is guarded by lakes and traps and requires a thoughtful approach.

Above: Perfectly manicured grass courts are part of the 20 court tennis complex at Marriott's Desert Springs.

Right: Swans are among the many exotic bird species that call Marriott's Desert Springs their home.

TURTLE BAY RESORT
PARADISE FOUND ON OAHU'S NORTH SHORE

Spread over 880 acres with five and a half miles of pristine white sand beaches and five secluded bays, Turtle Bay Resort is the jewel of Oahu's North Shore. With a recently completed $40 million renovation, Turtle Bay is a Mecca for outdoor recreation enthusiasts with two championship golf courses, world-class tennis facility and unlimited water sports including the world's most famous surfing venues– Sunset Beach, Waimea Bay and the Banzai Pipeline.

Turtle Bay Resort's two 18-hole golf courses, the Arnold Palmer Course and the Fazio Course, have been completely renovated with seashore paspalum to include tees, fairways and greens. The Palmer Course, designed by Arnold Palmer and Ed Seay, is the site of the PGA Senior Tour's Turtle Bay Championship. This Championship course plays to 7,199 yards and offering five sets of tees on

each hole, and in some cases six, to ensure that the course is challenging and can be enjoyed by players of all skill levels. The front nine offers a links-style layout while the back nine plays through a truly tropical setting wrapped around natural tidal pools and ponds and skirting the shoreline. The course forms a horseshoe around 100 acres of unspoiled wetlands.

The Fazio Course has hosted the LPGA Tour's Hawaiian Open and was also the site of the first Senior Skins Game. Three sets of tees are offered with the course playing to 6,535 yards. The course is George Fazio's only golf course in Hawaii and offers generous fairways, large deep bunkers and immaculately sculpted greens. The Fazio Course offers a wide variety of shot-making opportunities and breathtaking vistas of tropical hillsides and mountains and the Pacific Ocean.

Left: The par 3, 166 yard 11th hole on Turtle Bay's Fazio Course with the Pacific Ocean as a back drop on a typical day with the tradewinds blowing right to left.

Turtle Bay Resort, with its Five and a Half Acres of Secluded Shoreline, is the Jewel of Oahu's North Shore...

At Turtle Bay Resort the spirit of aloha beckons, the fragrance of tropical flowers fills the air, and sound of the surf in Turtle Bay heightens the senses. You can indulge every notion of a tropical paradise—majestic waterfalls, impossibly blue lagoons and lush rain forests that echo with the song of exotic birds all on the north shore.

Hawaiian legend refers to three men who walked "Kuilima" (to go arm-in-arm) while walking the shoreline of what is now resort

grounds, thus naming the area Kuilima. The hotel stands today on Kuilima Point which was considered a sacred place by Hawaiian Fishermen who erected an altar on the site. Relics from the altar are on exhibit at the world-renown Bishop Museum in Honolulu.

Turtle Bay, named for the green sea turtles always visible along the shore, is a popular surf area to the south of the hotel with three breaks that are best left to the experienced surfer. To the north, Kuilima Cove, offers quiet and gentle waters once known as the "little pool" and were a favorite swimming hole for Queen Liliuokalani when she was a young girl.

Above: Kawela Bay, southernmost of the resort's five bays, is bordered by a tropical jungle in its natural state.

Left: The par 3, 154 yard, 2nd hole on the Fazio Course with view across the lake to the Punamano Mountains.

In addition to the championship golf courses, the resort offers a wealth of outdoor activities including ten tennis courts, four lit for night play, and two tropically landscaped swimming pools. Snorkeling, surfing, kayaking, shoreline horseback riding and hiking add adventure to your experience at Turtle Bay. Along the North Shore coastline are some of the world's most legendary surfing spots– Sunset Beach, Banzai Pipeline and Waimea Bay– with winter waves up to 50 feet breaking offshore.

Clockwise from right: An aerial view of Turtle Bay Resort's 10 tennis courts. The shoreline of Kawela Bay, the western boundary of the resort. A surfer in the barrel at Pipeline.

Below: The par 4, 452 yard 17th hole on the Palmer Course.

With the hotel perched on the peninsula at Kuilima Point every one of the resort's 375 guest rooms, 26 suites and 42 beachfront cottages enjoy spectacular views of the surrounding Pacific Ocean. The rooms are beautifully appointed and feature the latest amenities including air conditioning and private lanais.

Dining at the resort is an experience one will not soon forget. Palm Terrace has casual dining for breakfast, lunch and dinner daily, 21 Degrees North offers fine dining serving a delicious Hawaiian regional cuisine menu and the Surf Room serves a memorable Sunday Brunch among swaying palms and gentle ocean breezes.

Minutes from the resort are the sugar plantation villages of Kahuku and the famous Polynesian Cultural Center. Turtle Bay is a scenic 40 mile drive from Honolulu International Airport.

Far left: Sunset over Turtle Bay from the picturesque Beach Cottages.

Left: The par 4, 403 yard 6th hole on the Fazio Course, the site of the first Senior Skins Game which included Arnold Palmer, Gary Player, Chi Chi Rodriques and Sam Snead.

Below: The par 3, 177 yard 15th hole on the Arnold Palmer Course.

RESORT AT SQUAW CREEK
Mountain Golf In Its Purest Tradition

Millions of years ago glacial ice carved this rugged mountain terrain in California's High Sierra, leaving behind a fertile valley full of wildflowers, ponderosa pine, deer and elk. Today, Squaw Valley is known around the world for its crystal-clear air, Olympic-class skiing and championship golf at The Resort at Squaw Creek.

Just minutes from the sandy beaches and glacial boulders of Lake Tahoe, The Resort at Squaw Creek is located at the site of the 1960 Winter Olympics... a year-round playground surrounded by 10,000-foot mountain peaks. The resort is situated at an elevation 6,200 feet. The heady, euphoric feeling guests talk about is partly the altitude and partly the elation of playing a magnificent golf course nestled in an alpine valley in the middle of the High Sierra.

The Resort at Squaw Creek Golf Course opened in 1992 and soon was named one of *Golf Digest's* "Top Five New Resort Courses." Famed golf course architect Robert Trent Jones, Jr. designed a links-style layout of traditional mountain golf which also has won accolades for its unique approach to environmental preservation. Utilizing only 80 acres of playable land, Squaw Creek presents golfers with the challenge of a narrow field of play and specific landing areas.

Above: The green on the 18th hole and the main pool and recreation area.

Left: A view from the 18th fairway to the par 4, 385 yard 10th hole.

Tees, fairways and greens at Squaw Creek have been carefully placed to preserve existing wetlands and forested hillsides. In some locations, the course blends so effortlessly with its surroundings it almost disappears into Squaw Valley's rugged alpine backdrop.

All 18 holes of Squaw Creek's championship course wrap around a horseshoe-shaped meadow surrounded by mountains on three sides. Five holes play into rather steep mountain terrain, while others play along natural wetlands and intimidating water hazards. As Robert Trent Jones, Jr. stated, "Accuracy, not length, will be definitely be at a premium on this golf course."

Beyond golf, there are endless ways to enjoy an invigorating mountain experience at The Resort at Squaw Creek. The hotel, with its Frank Lloyd Wright-inspired design, takes advantage of its alpine setting with ceiling high expanses of glass framing sweeping views of Squaw Valley. In the lobby, the warmth of a blazing fire takes the chill of a cool summer evening. Hotel accommodations include 403 custom guestrooms and suites, some with fireplaces, and all with panoramic windows that open to the fresh mountain air.

All year long, guests soak and swim in the resort's scenic outdoor water garden, with its three pools, spas, waterfall and waterslide. Squaw Creek's own Spa and Fitness Center is designed for the personal attention and pampering that guests expect– our signature

Tahoe hot stone massage, a quick workout or the relaxation of a redwood sauna. Five distinctive restaurants are situated conveniently throughout the resort grounds and offer expertly prepared cuisine, from pastries and deli sandwiches at Sweet Potatoes to four-diamond gourmet California cuisine at elegant Glissandi.

Clockwise from above left: The pristine waters of Lake Tahoe. The lodge, pool and spa area behind the green of the par 4, 2nd hole. Squaw Creek on a late afternoon in spring.

Left: A hot-air balloon hovers above the 6th green on the par 3, 210 yard 6th hole.

The crisp mountain air of Squaw Valley encourages outdoor activities– horseback riding along Squaw Creek, mountain biking, croquet on the hotel lawn or a game of tennis at the resort's Tennis Center. Fly fishing and day hiking are popular pastimes for locals and visitors alike. Nearby Lake Tahoe, Nevada, offers gambling, shopping and non-stop night life. For a more reflective time, take a quiet boat cruise on the crystal-clear waters of Lake Tahoe, which are the world's 10th deepest, with 72 miles of meandering shoreline.

In all seasons, The Resort at Squaw Creek reflects the essence of a High Sierra experience with protected wetlands, towering granite peaks, meadows resplendent with wildflowers and the scent of fresh pine. This is mountain golf at its very best.

Top: A father and son walking to the green on the 1st hole on a summer morning.

Right: The par 5, 514 yard, dogleg left 9th hole.

Far right: The par 4, 406 yard 1st hole among the granite peaks of Squaw Valley, site of the 1960 Winter Olympic Games.

SUPERSTITION MOUNTAIN
GOLF AND COUNTRY CLUB

Jack Nicklaus & Lyle Anderson Golf at the Base of Arizona's Legendary Superstition Mountain Range...

In all the Southwest, the Superstition Mountains have no rival. Their imposing height and rugged visage form a backdrop that causes you to pause and marvel at nature's extravagance. When exploring this land, you will walk in the footsteps of ancient Native Americans whose petroglyphs are vivid reminders of the mysterious history that abounds in this beautiful place. Spanish conquistador Coronado passed through this area during the 16th century, searching for the Seven Cities of Cibola. Legends suggest that in the 1880s, Jacob Waltz, the famous "Dutchman," found Coronado's elusive gold, but took its location to his death. The Lost Dutchman Mine remains undiscovered.

The real treasures of these mountains today are the magnificent vistas visible from the Superstition Mountain Clubhouse and its two championship golf courses.

Right: The par 4, 419 yard 1st hole on the Prospector course framed against a backdrop of the Sonoran Desert and the rugged Superstition Mountains.

Above: A view of the west side of the Superstition Mountain Clubhouse across the green of the par 4, 442 yard 9th hole on the Prospector course.

Superstition Mountain Golf and Country Club is a private, gated community spread over 890 desert landscaped acres in the Sonoran Desert foothills of the Superstition Mountains in Superstition Mountain, Arizona. The community features 36 holes of private Nicklaus– designed golf, a Clubhouse situated in the heart of the community, a planned Sports Club and variety of interesting home options including luxurious villas, custom homes and home sites. When this meticulously designed distinctive community is completed, more than half of its 890 acres will remain open space.

Since 1982, The Lyle Anderson Company, Inc. of Scottsdale, Arizona has been developing premier golf communities that continue to exceed expectations. Desert Highlands and

Desert Mountain in Scottsdale; Las Campanas in Santa Fe, New Mexico; Hokuli'a on the Kona Coast of Hawaii's Big Island, and now Superstition Mountain Golf and Country Club in Phoenix's East Valley are a testament to the company's long-term commitment to sensitive planning, unsurpassed amenities and outstanding golf. Attention to detail and creative development concepts have made The Lyle Anderson Companies one of

the world's leading land developers. In all of the company's projects,

including the Loch Lomand Golf Club in Scotland, development experience,

The two 18 hole Jack Nicklaus designed championship golf courses, Prospector and Lost Gold, are nestled along the base of the legendary Superstition Mountains. Prospector is the more forgiving of the two courses, with wide fairways and a variety of tees, while the Lost Gold course is playable by all skill levels but features smaller greens and deeper bunkers. The Prospector course, at 7,193 yards, was designed by Jack Nicklaus and his son Gary. The course was the host of the nationally televised 2002 SENIOR PGA's Major Championship– The Countrywide *Tradition*. The

superior maintenance and hands-on management have lead to unparalled facilities that provide premier golf experiences for members, friends and family.

A twenty-plus year relationship between Lyle Anderson and Jack Nicklaus has resulted in the superb courses found at the company developments in the United States and an architect / developer interface capable of flawless execution from design through construction.

Club also has made a commitment to organize and operate the finest

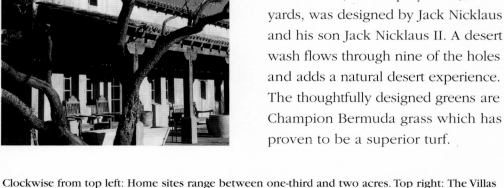

Junior Golf Program available at any private club. The Juniors play on the Cubby Course, an alternative set of tees, created on the Prospector course with a yardage of 2,839 and a par of 72.

Lost Gold, which plays at 7,351 yards, was designed by Jack Nicklaus and his son Jack Nicklaus II. A desert wash flows through nine of the holes and adds a natural desert experience. The thoughtfully designed greens are Champion Bermuda grass which has proven to be a superior turf.

Clockwise from top left: Home sites range between one-third and two acres. Top right: The Villas at Golden Eagle Village. Above right: The par 5, 553 yard 18th hole on Prospector during the 2002 Tradition. Above left: The Carriage House. Left: The par 4, 370 yard 15th hole on Prospector.

Superstition Mountain Golf and Country Club offers either golf or social memberships for those who are approved by the membership committee. Both memberships include access to the Clubhouse, certainly one of the most beautifully appointed and constructed in the country, and the planned Sports Club. The Clubhouse features food and beverage service in the Restaurant, a private dining room and outdoor dining terraces, men's and ladies locker rooms, a

After playing his first round on Prospector, Jack stated, "This is the finest conditioned course I've ever played."

Jack Nicklaus

of the region's leading design and construction firms. A Design Center is also offered for property owners to customize their interior finishes from an impressive collection of designer materials.

The Villas at Golden Eagle Village feature four different four plans in a total of 65 villas located between the 9th and 10th fairways of the Prospector course. The homes at Sunset village offer four different floorplans on one-third acre parcels along the par 3, 192 yard 17th hole of the Prospector course.

Superstition Mountain Golf and Country Club was acknowledged for excellence in private residential

library with a meeting room and full service golf shop with the latest in equipment and apparel.

Superstition Mountain's ownership opportunities are exciting and diverse.

custom home sites range in size from one-third of an acre to two acres and offer inspiring views that include the golf courses, mountains, natural desert or city lights. The community offers a Featured Builder Program to provide owners with access to many

community design at the 2001 Gold Nugget Awards with four merit awards going to The Villas at Golden Eagle Village and a Grand Award to the Cetona model. In 1999 the Ranch House, which is truly inspiring, won a Grand Award.

Above: An aerial view of the par 3, 184 yard 4th hole on the Prospector course.

Left: The Tuscany inspired Superstition Mountain Clubhouse is reflected in the lake guarding the green on the par 5, 553 yard 18th hole on Prospector.

HOKULI'A

Jack Nicklaus & Lyle Anderson Golf on the Big Island's Kona Coast...

Rich in the heritage, legends and lore of Hawaii, the "Big Island of Hawaii," also known as "The Orchid Island," presents perhaps the truest Hawaiian experience. With a land area of 4,038 square miles, the island of Hawaii is the southernmost island in the Hawaiian Archipelago. Along a secluded three-mile stretch of The Big Island's Kona Coast, you'll discover land that has gone untouched for 200 years. Before that, it had been a playground for the Hawaiians for centuries. You can still find petroglyphs, monuments and other ancient Hawaiian treasures nearby.

The spirit of Aloha and the timeless magic of old Hawaii is captured in a most luxurious and gracious manner at Hokuli'a, which translates as "Star of Desire." Located on 1,550 acres just south of historic Kailua-Kona on the Kona Coast, Hokuli'a is Hawaii's first totally private golf community.

Left: The par 4, 482 yard 2nd hole is a sweeping dogleg left, protected on the right by a freshwater lake, that leads to the ocean shoreline.

Above: Waves crash on lava cliffs at Hokuli'a's 140 acre Shoreline Park.

Hokuli'a is the latest creation of Lyle Anderson, one of the most celebrated luxury community developers, and Jack Nicklaus, one of the most renowned golf course designers in the world. Hokuli'a's three miles of spectacular oceanfront climbs gently to 1,250 feet giving virtually every homesite a spectacular view of the ocean. The average summer temperature is 77° F and falls to 72° F in the winter. Water off the coast is always in the upper 70s and soft breezes average 5mph. A truly tranquil setting with perfect weather year-round.

The par-72 Jack Nicklaus Signature golf course measures 7,335 yards from the Nicklaus tees and creates a centerpiece for the community while the Pacific Ocean provides a dramatic backdrop. The eleventh collaboration between Jack Nicklaus and Lyle Anderson, the goal at Hokuli'a has been to create the finest residential private oceanside golf community in the world with one of the world's top golf courses. The golf course was built with three goals in mind;

to be among the most beautiful golf courses golfers have ever played; to be very playable, and to be exclusive to provide easy access for the club's members.

Top left: The par 3, 222 yard 8th hole. Above: The par 4, 361 yard 12th hole is completely guarded by sculpted bunkers.

Below: The par 3, 192 yard 3rd hole is all carry.

"Hokuli'a compares favorably to many Nicklaus designs. Overall, it takes a back seat to none."

Jack Nicklaus

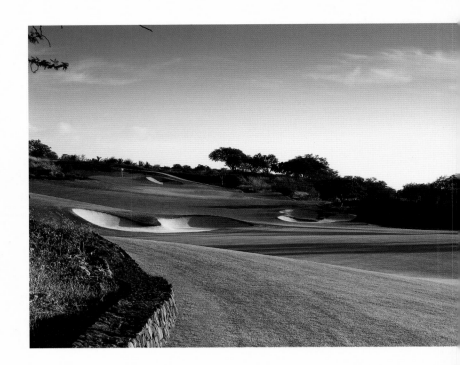

The clubhouse at Hokuli'a is being designed as a series of Hawaiian pavilions to capture the ambiance of the island with views of the 18th hole, surrounding tropical landscape and stunning sunsets off the Kona Coast. Here, Hokuli'a's members and guests are treated to open-air dining platforms, interior gardens, a secluded library, wine room, men's and women's locker rooms and indoor/outdoor men's and women's lanais and terraces. The club offers casual and fine dining with the Pavilion's world-class gourmet chef Peter Abacar (who trained under award winning chef Alan Wong), a spa with private treatment

bungalows and tennis courts.

The Hokuli'a Beach Club is planned to be a perfect spot for casual dining. Fresh and salt-water pools offer a day of fun in the sun for the entire family. Some of the best Marlin fishing in the world is right off the coast of Hokuli'a and two club owned boats are available to take advantage of the world-class sportfishing as well as other water activities including scuba diving, snorkeling and shoreline cruises.

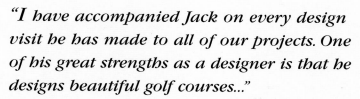

"I have accompanied Jack on every design visit he has made to all of our projects. One of his great strengths as a designer is that he designs beautiful golf courses..."

Lyle Anderson

Homesites at Hokuli'a range from one to three acres, more than large enough to allow privacy and flexibility of home design and orientation, and are priced between $1 million and $8 million, depending upon location. All homesite buyers receive an equity membership in the club which transfers with the sale of the homesite. At Hokuli'a homeowners can design and build their homes on their homesites whenever they wish, unlike most other planned communities there are no penalties for building at your own pace.

Lyle Anderson knew instinctively that attention to native heritage would be of the utmost importance in the ultimate success of Hokuli'a. "The name Hokuli'a, meaning "Star of Desire," has ties to the generations of Hawaiians who have navigated the island waters," Lyle said. "We feel the name conveys the aura of tranquility and the promise that one senses at the property, as well as its rich sense

of history. Our company is determined, through the ambiance and architecture, to capture and incorporate the sense of history and culture that the property has been part of for centuries."

Top left: The par 5, 525 yard 9th hole plays uphill from your approach shot over two fairway bunkers to a green guarded at the right front.

Above: Sunset at The Pavilion at Hokuli'a. The Pavilion is adjacent to the 10th green and reflects a true island ambiance.

Left: The par 4, 441 yard, 10th hole where golfers are rewarded with spectacular ocean views upon arriving at the green.

MARRIOTT'S
SHADOW RIDGE

Nick Faldo Championship Golf in Palm Desert, California...

Marriott's Shadow Ridge Resort is located just two hours from Southern California's major metropolitan areas in Palm Desert. The Resort, with its sunny days and crystal-clear nights, is certain to dazzle the senses. Encompassing 312 acres of unspoiled desert, Shadow Ridge has been artfully designed to create a relaxing and entertaining vacation experience in one of the best year-round climates found anywhere. The city of Palm Desert offers visitors many world class restaurants, elegant shopping plazas, diverse nightlife and a wealth of outdoor recreational activities and cultural events.

Left: The left side of the fairway on the par 4, 417 yard 9th hole is guarded by a stream and waterfalls. The green is protected by a lake. A well placed second shot is crucial.

97

The Resort at Shadow Ridge features many amenities including resort-style swimming pools, a children's activity center, tennis courts and a fitness center. The luxurious villas tucked among the fairways offer full kitchens, a living and dining room and a washer and dryer. Each of the fully-equipped two bedroom two bath villas offer lake, mountain or fairway views. Resort dining options include the Cielo, The Bunker, a poolside bar and grill and The Marketplace store and deli.

The 7,006 yard, par 71, championship 18 hole golf course was Nick Faldo's first design in the United States. Faldo, winner of six major golf championships, teamed up with Marriott to create a completely different type desert golf course, where his passion for strategic design and international experience are clearly evident. The course is set against the backdrop of the

often snow-capped Santa Rosa Mountains and features generous fairways and bold bunkers.

Shadow Ridge also features the third Faldo Golf Institute by Marriott, perhaps the most comprehensive learning center in the country. A variety of instructional programs are available to meet the needs of students at any skill level.

Offering superb privacy and personal amenities the Villas are a luxurious home-away-from-home in spectacular Palm Desert. Here, owners and guests are sure to experience something wonderful, whether lakes, waterfalls, fairways or mountains, at every vista refreshing the spirit in this tranquil environment.

Above: The par 4, 404 yard 4th hole.

Far left: The par 3, 174 yard 17th hole with the snow-capped peaks of Mt. San Jacinto rising from the desert floor.

Left: Sunrise on the par 4, 423 yard, 10th hole at Shadow Ridge.

Below: A stream wanders from the green through the fairway to the tees on the par 4, 461 yard 18th hole, adding tranquility and an extra element of challenge.

RAVEN GOLF CLUB AT THREE PEAKS

A Magnificent Blend of Brilliant Golf Design and the Natural Wonders of the Rocky Mountains...

T he Raven at Three Peaks will stimulate your senses in every conceivable way. Designed by Hurdzan-Fry Golf Design and PGA touring professional Tom Lehman, the golf course is surrounded by the vast beauty of Colorado's Rocky Mountains. This course will leave you wishing for another nine holes, and three more rolls of film, at the end of your round. Located in Silverthorne, Colorado, Three Peaks is the consummate challenge for the advanced player as well as the occasional weekender.

At 7,413 yards in length, the course was designed to play with varying degrees of challenge from each tee. The routing of Three Peaks minimizes the steepness of the natural terrain while preserving the character of the topography, resulting in elevation changes with level landing areas and green complexes. When a course is built on mountain slopes architects must take into consideration the additional distance the ball will soar at higher altitudes. Added flight is either a blessing for straight shots, or a curse for those that stray off-line. Knowing this, the architects designed the course to compensate for the additional distance.

Above: The 8th hole, *Buena Vista*, a 184 yard, par 3 with breathtaking views.
Right: Accuracy is a premium on *Monte Cristo*, the par 4, 415 yard 15th hole which is heavily guarded by bunkers.

> *"The end result is spectacular. The property at Three Peaks is perfect for a great golf course."*
>
> Tom Lehman

Among the distinguishing features of the design at the Raven at Three Peaks are unique bunkering patterns. Influenced by the legendary design traits of Dr. Alister MacKenzie, the bunkers are rugged with long grass and vegetation growing around the edges, thus creating a distinctive look and feel to the golf course. "They are not only aesthetically pleasing," says Director of Golf Rick Fretland, "but a challenge as well for our guests who find themselves in the midst of these hazards."

Each hole at Three Peaks has its own distinctive personality. The par 4, 426 yard 1st hole, named *Hi-Ho*, opens with a wide fairway and closes with a well-contoured green neighboring a pond to the left and rear of the green with bunkers protecting the putting surface from both sides. Behind the green, birdhouses are mounted to enhance the natural habitat for swallow and mountain bluebirds. *Wild Irishman*, the par 5, 587 yard, 2nd hole, stretches through high mountain grasslands and introduces golfers to the pleasures of hitting the ball at a high altitude. If closely observed, a pair of nesting osprey can be seen atop a pole near the green. The osprey have been returning to this nesting place since 1982 and are often seen fishing for trout in the nearby Blue River.

The 10th hole, *Orphan Boy*, is a 376 yard, par 4, that presents a birdie opportunity as long as you avoid the fairway bunkers to the left and right from an elevated tee. A precision approach is critical to the deep false-fronted green. *Waterloo*, the par 5, 599 yard 11th hole, requires a long tee shot followed by a second shot that is all carry over a large lake in front of the green. The safe play here is to lay-up.

The par 4, 418 yard 7th hole, *Silver Spoon*, may tempt some to cut the dogleg for a closer approach to the green, which is well-protected by deep bunkers.

The 213 yard, par 3, 14th hole captures the spirit of Three Peaks. A picture-perfect green setting, wetlands and a lake between the tee and green, this hole personifies mountain golf with the Gore Mountain Range visible in the distance. Stop, look, listen and take it all in. Its no wonder the hole is named *Silence*.

Monte Cristo, the par 4, 415 yard 15th hole, puts a premium on accuracy. With fairway bunkers to the right and wildflowers and native vegetation to the left, both areas are best left alone. The green is guarded by a creek crossing the front and a bunker. On this hole it's fairway and green only. Miss one or the other and a challenge awaits you.

Far left: The 213 yard, par 3, 14th hole, *Silence,* plays across wetlands and a pond that provides habitat for wood ducks.

Left: *Warriors Mark*, the 543 yard par 5 6th hole, offers a chance for birdie if you can avoid the bunkers to the left, right and center of the fairway along with those to the right and left of the green.

Below: *King Solomon*, the par 5, 601 yard 16th hole, is a long downhill hole that doglegs to the right.

"I'm very happy with the outcome of this golf course," said Tom Lehman. "Michael Hurdzan, Dana Fry and I worked very hard to design a golf course that would be a memorable experience for everyone who comes here. I think we have done just that." Dana Fry adds, "The scenery is breathtaking in every direction and we had very high expectations for the design of the course. Looking at the completed project, it's apparent that our expectations have been exceeded."

The golf course and setting speak for themselves, but what makes the experience at Three Peaks truly exclusive is Intrawest Golf's premier trademark known as the Raven brand. Throughout North America, Raven branded courses have garnered a strong reputation for providing high-end memorable golf experiences. Each component of guest satisfaction must pass strict criteria to be considered a Raven Golf Club, including guest services, food and beverage,

Right: *Orphan Boy,* the 367 yard, par 4, 10th hole, has an uphill approach to a deep green with a false front.

maintenance and management. "The course will challenge any guest," said Lehman. "But more importantly, with the commitment to service, course conditioning and dedication to guest satisfaction by the Raven staff, this will be an experience long remembered after the round is completed."

"By blending tradition and modern styling with the design of the bunkers and wide fairways in a mountain setting we have created a truly unique golf course with challenges, rewards and options for every golfer," says director of golf Rick Fretland. "And combined with the Raven name and quality, I think we've created the ideal mountain golf experience." It seems those words are traveling fast. In 2000, with the course open for just a month, Three Peaks was awarded honorable mention among the "Top Ten Courses You Can Play" by *Golf Magazine*.

Experience golf for the senses and you will discover the myriad reasons The Raven Golf Club at Three Peaks is now one of the most anticipated golf destinations in Colorado.

Top: The rocky creek dissecting the fairway on the 468 yard 17th hole, *Last Dollar*, works to control erosion and sediment build up from mountain runoff.

Above: Trapper Rudd, the owner of Cutthroat Anglers in Silverthorne, takes a local trout.

Left: *Monte Cristo*, the par 4, 415 yard 15th hole, is fronted by a mountain stream and a cavernous bunker.

COPPER MOUNTAIN

Year-round Vacation Headquarters in the Heart of the Rockies...

Copper Mountain Resort, located in the heart of the majestic Rocky Mountains in Colorado, was once just a sleepy little day ski area but has grown over the years into one of Colorado's premier year-round destination resorts. Summer activities include golf at Copper Creek Golf Club, chair lift rides up the mountain, hiking, mountain biking down the ski runs and fishing in Ten Mile Creek to name just a few. Winter brings some of the best skiing and snowboarding terrain in the United States.

The Copper Creek championship golf course, designed by Pete and Perry Dye, is located just steps away from the East Village at the base of Copper Mountain Resort. The course, at an elevation of 9,700 feet, is America's highest championship golf club. With fantastic views of the Ten Mile Range, Copper Creek's par 70, 6,070 yard layout is one of the most beautiful in Summit County.

Above: The East Village at Copper Mountain Resort in summer.

Left: The par 4, 482 yard 2nd hole with the Ten Mile Range in the distance.

The Copper Mountain ski area was originally developed by Chuck Lewis in 1971. Lewis negotiated a deal to purchase 280 acres at the base of the mountain and worked with the Forest Service to establish the parameters and guidelines for the ski area. During the summer of 1971 the initial construction began on the ski trails. Copper has since grown to its current size of 2,450 skiable acres and gained the status of Summit County's largest ski area. The mountain has 23 lifts: 1 six-person high speed, 4 high-speed quads, 5 triples, 5 doubles and 8 surface lifts, combined capable of moving 30,630 skiers per hour. The mountain receives an average annual snowfall of 280 inches and is capable of making snow on 400 acres. Of the resort's 125 trails 21% are offered for beginners, 25% for intermediate,

36% for advanced and 18% for expert skiers with the longest run covering 2.8 miles.

The Copper Ski and Snowboard School offers a variety of programs for skiers and snowboarders. Lesson options include private lessons, level buster, adult group lessons and Copper kids. A private lesson offers the student either a half or full day at their own pace; the level buster lasts three days and guarantees progress to another level; the adult group last a half day and the Copper kids takes place at the Schoolhouse where everything is kid-sized and kids up to 13 years old are grouped by age and ability.

Copper Mountain Resort features the Copper Villages offering a choice of two unique villages— the New Village and the East Village. The New Village is a bustling, slope side, high alpine village that's in the heart of it all. Located at the base of the blue terrain, with easy access to all of the black and green runs and a lift or shuttle ride away from the family area at Union Creek, the New Village in the summer time is a scenic walking space lined with great shops, restaurants and gathering places. The East Village offers a wide variety of lodging choices, including large and impressive mountain homes with spectacular views

of Ten Mile Range. The East Village most easily accesses expert and intermediate terrain from Colorado's first six-person, high-speed lift, the Super Bee, but beginner terrain is not far away by using our complimentary shuttle system. Both villages offer a wide variety of lodging choices from five bedroom mountain homes to hotel rooms.

Top left: The view from the top of the quad lift above the New Village.

Top right: The quad lift above the New Village speeds skiers to the mountain in winter and to a variety of outdoor activities in summer.

Above: Trapper Rudd, owner of Cutthroat Anglers in Silverthorne, plies the waters of Ten Mile Creek.

Left: The par 4, 441 yard, 6th hole at Copper Creek Golf Club.

WOLF CREEK
GOLF RESORT

Nature preserved while creating one of the Top Three Golf Courses in America

The Wolf Creek golf course at Paradise Canyon was designed by Dennis Rider and co-designer Jon Rider, Dennis' son, using nature as their guide. No drawings were used to design the golf course holes before construction began, just a mental sketch in Dennis' mind. The focus was on two prime directives– create one of the best golf experiences in the world, while preserving the natural environment in such a geologically fragile region that a construction worker's footsteps may take years to disappear.

Dennis worked alongside the bulldozers and tractors each day, thus allowing the land to design the course and protecting the site from any over-zealous activities. The result was a golf course that surpasses most existing courses while retaining the natural landscape of Paradise Canyon. Wolf Creek was awarded honors as one of the **"Top Three Golf Courses in America"** by *Golf Digest* in January of 2002.

Above: Wolf Creek flows along the backside of the 17th green.

Left: The par 4, 390 yard, 9th hole drive is full-carry across the lake.

Golf course design, practiced at its highest levels, requires a wide variety of club selection and numerous shot challenges to play. Wolf Creek at Paradise Canyon is certainly no exception to the rule with shot making challenges that bring every club out of the bag. The extreme measures Dennis and Jon Rider took to build Wolf Creek without disturbing natural desert terrain, sandstone cliffs and native flora and fauna is evident everywhere one looks. Grass was grown from

turf rather than seeds and the Riders kept heavy machinery off the grass by filling the bunkers with a blend of crushed white marble and sand flown in by helicopter.

The Riders, in their joint roles of developers and course designers, worked to ensure proper handling of the area's wildlife which includes coyote, jackrabbit, roadrunner, desert tortoise and chipmunk. These extra precautions pushed costs on the Wolf Creek project to around $50 million, but created a unique world-class golf environment.

Above: A migrating Wood Duck, *Aix sponsa*, enjoys the pristine waters of Wolf Creek.

Right: The par 3, 248 yard 8th hole features an island green surrounded by Wolf Creek.

The par 72 Wolf Creek at Paradise Canyon course features five sets of tees; the Challenger at 7,018 yards, Champions at 6,370 yards, Masters at 5,780 yards, Signature at 5,211 yards and Classic at 4,169 yards, allowing a challenge for low-handicap golfers while affording pleasant experiences for the higher handicap players. The USGA rated the course as the third toughest in the United States from the Challenger tees.

The course winds through desert canyons among cliffs and boulders and features six lakes, seven waterfalls and a half-mile long waterway, Wolf Creek. The Wolf Creek course pumps more cubic feet of water, with more elevation change, than any other golf course in America.

The Bermuda grass fairways, tees and rough, and the bent grass greens, are beautifully manicured and add a sharp contrast to the spectacular sandstone of the canyon walls. In the winter months, the course is re-seeded in its entirety, including roughs, bunker collars and grassy natural areas. The course's water features continually flow from lake-to-lake carried naturally by the reconstructed Wolf Creek, which has become a rich habitat for wildlife

including migratory waterfowl, quail and an abundance of chukar.

place, he accepted the challenge that a number of holes might be deemed

extreme elevation changes such as the 3rd hole, a 227 yard, par 3 that plays uphill with carry across a canyon. When you reach the green, you are on one of the highest points on the course and are rewarded with 360° views. On the par 4, 445 yard, 2nd hole you will drive your tee shot from a tee box that stands 11 stories tall:

While Dennis Rider was determined to leave the natural landforms in

non-traditional. The resulting design has created spectacular holes with

Far left: View of the 7th green from the elevated 5th hole tees.

Left: The 12th green across the lake and the 13th hole up the canyon.

Below: The green on the 304 yard, par 4, 7th hole looking across to the 6th fairway.

The trio of the 16th, 17th and 18th holes takes you through all the course's elevation changes in three holes. The 16th, a 395 yard par 4, is crafted on one of the highest ridges on the course. From the elevated tees of the par 5, 560 yard 17th hole vistas of three states come into view, with Utah and Arizona to the left and the

"I wanted to create a course that would be a masterpiece... yet I was wary of leaving a single footprint in the canyon's natural areas."

Dennis Rider, Course Designer

High above the ninth hole are the Golf Villas. Streamside homes and villas line the banks of Cascade stream, both projects were developed by Dennis Rider and are available for purchase or lodging for golf groups.

Wolf Creek at Paradise Canyon is located just one hour north of Las Vegas, Nevada.

mountains of Nevada straight ahead and to the right. The second and third shots are both over water to an island green on the canyon floor. The 18th hole, a 370 yard par 4, brings you back to the top of the canyon walls finishing on a green surrounded by waterfalls on three sides with a steep cliff to the right.

Wolf Creek at Paradise Canyon's 17,200 square-foot clubhouse contains Baileyi, a gourmet restaurant and intimate bar with breathtaking views of the surrounding terrain, and the Wolf Creek golf shop. The golf shop carries all the necessities including top of the line equipment, quality apparel, jewelry and art.

Above: The golf villas and clubhouse sit high above the 390 yard, par 4, 9th hole in this view from the tees across the lake.

Far left: The 472 yard, par 4, 10th hole plays uphill and is well guarded by bunkers to the left side of the green.

Upper left: The 17th hole, a 560 yard par 5, plays from elevated tees. The second shot carries Wolf Creek and the third shot is to an island green.

"One of the Top Three Golf Courses in Hawaii."

Golf Digest

KOʻOLAU GOLF CLUB

The World's Most Challenging Golf Course Awaits the Fearless on the Island of Oahu.

Koʻolau Golf Club, located on the beautiful windward side of the island of Oahu, is considered the most challenging golf course in the world. Carved from a magnificent tropical forest on the side of the 2,000 foot high Koʻolau mountain range, the course encompasses three distinct climate zones and features dramatic vistas of the rain forest and the Pacific Ocean. The club's facilities include an 18 hole championship golf course, a spacious 125,000 square foot clubhouse and a 5-acre grass practice facility. Adding to the breathtaking views and great golf experience golfers share the property with a variety of indigenous and imported wildlife including feral pigs, Jackson's chameleons and an impressive variety of birds.

Koʻolau was designed by renowned architects Dick Nugent and Jack Tuthill. The 7,310 yard, par 72 layout features cascading waterfalls, winding ravines and an abundance of lush native vegetation. The greens are Seashore Paspalum turf grass which offers a world-class quality putting surface all year round. Even though the course is considered extremely challenging, with four sets of tees Koʻolau promises an enjoyable experience for golfers of any skill level.

Above: Tee shots on the par 5, 593 yard 1st hole need to be carefully placed to avoid six strategically positioned fairway bunkers.

Left: The par 4, 476 yard 18th hole is one of the world's most dramatic finishing holes. From the tee what appears to be bushes and trees behind the green is actually a three-canopy rain forest with trees hundreds of feet high.

The course's Aloha Academy of Golf offers a variety of programs for juniors, women and families. The teaching and practice facilities feature state-of-the-art video and computer equipment, grass practice tees and manicured chipping/putting practice greens. Private, semi-private and group lessons are offered for locals and visitors of all skill levels by PGA and LPGA instructors. Global Positioning Satellite systems are installed on all golf carts and club rental and fitting is available.

Ko'olau has three varieties of memberships with privileges including personal lockers and

"One of the Top 100 Places You Can Play."
Golf Magazine

golf bag storage; use of men's and women's locker rooms featuring a Sauna and Euro Bath; use of the game room featuring a billiards table, television and other gaming tables; preferred tee times, and participation in monthly golf tournaments and other exclusive events.

From golf outings and group tournaments to weddings, corporate retreats, business meetings and seminars, Ko'olau Golf Club's unparalleled facilities and world-class service in one of the most stunning locations in the world are a hard combination to beat. The 125,000 square foot clubhouse features 13,000 square feet of banquet facilities including the signature "Glass Ballroom" and traditional Grand Ballroom; first class men's and women's locker and lounge facilities, and the *Honey's at Ko'olau* restaurant. Honey's was named after Honey Ho, a kupuna

from Kaneohe whose *Honey's* restaurant was popular with locals, tourists and the military for more than 39 years and was the birthplace of Honey's son, Don Ho. The restaurant offers Continental and Pacific-Asian cuisine, a warm Hawaiian atmosphere and Sunday Brunch.

Top left: The 125,000 square foot clubhouse.

Top right: The par 4, 373 yard 15th hole is carved into the side of the Ko'olau mountain range.

Above: The green of the par 5, 567 yard 16th hole.

Left: The par 4, 442 yard 3rd hole.

MARRIOTT
GRAND RESIDENCE CLUB
AND
TIMBER LODGE, LAKE TAHOE

Edgewood Golf, Heavenly® Skiing and the Bluest Lake in the World...

Lake Tahoe has represented the ideal retreat since the late 1800s, a favorite summer and winter retreat for generations. Interest hit an all time high after the 1960 Winter Olympics were held at nearby Squaw Valley. Lake Tahoe became a timeless retreat known for its outdoor summer activities centered around the waters of the world's second largest alpine lake and winter sports venues that are among the most exciting in North America.

Marriott Grand Residence Club was created as a unique vacation home where residents enjoy the Lake Tahoe lifestyle year-round. Activities are as abundant as the scenic vistas. The alpine village surrounding the resort is complete with cinema-plex theaters, exciting dining choices, shopping and an ice skating rink. Both Marriott Grand Residence Club and Marriott's Timber Lodge are located at the base of Heavenly® Ski Resort, a year-round destination for active vacationers, and within walking distance of Lake Tahoe and its beaches, casinos and world-class entertainment.

Above: Marriott Grand Residence Club, South Lake Tahoe, California.

Right: The par 5, 572 yard 18th hole at the Edgewood Tahoe Golf Course is guarded by Lake Tahoe on the right and a lake on the left.

Marriott Grand Residence Club represents a unique opportunity for second home ownership within an exciting alpine village that features all of the benefits and amenities of a fine resort hotel. Enjoy concierge services, valet and daily housekeeping along with a private health club and spa. Grand Residence Club is a cornerstone of Park Avenue's redevelopment project within the new Heavenly Village. The Residences use unconventional shapes, with areas such as kitchens, bathrooms and bedrooms tucked into niches. A typical Residence contains a central living room / dining room / kitchen area that is flanked by two bedrooms.

Far left: A young golfer in a bunker on the par 4, 434 yard 13th hole.

Left: The par 4, 441 yard 10th hole. Edgewood is a George Fazio course refined in recent years by his nephew, Tom Fazio.

Residences vary considerably in size from 400-square foot studios to penthouses of 2,000 plus square feet and can be either a single story or two stories. Each of the Residences is wired for cable television, telephones

Edgewood Tahoe has been consistently rated as "One of the Top 100 Golf Courses" by Golf Digest.

and internet access. With a variety of ownership plans available, Marriott Grand Residence Club offers a second home that is second to none with the utmost in flexibility.

The Edgewood Tahoe golf course is built along the south shore of Lake Tahoe and is arguably one of the most scenic golf courses in the world. Edgewood has a long history dating back to 1896 when the Park family purchased Friday's Station, which served as a stage line for both the Wells Fargo Express and the Pony Express, and the surrounding ranch land. Brooks Park had the vision to create a world-class

golf property on land along the lake that once was used to graze cattle. The

course, which opened in 1968, was designed by George Fazio with his

Timber Lodge's Villas range in size from one to two bedrooms capable of accommodating up to 8 guests. Villa amenities include fully equipped kitchens with granite counter tops and premium appliances, living and dining areas, bathrooms with granite counter tops and a soaking tub in the master bath. The resort offers residents a central courtyard pool with a children's pool and whirlpool spas, a fitness center, a children's activity center, a restaurant, The MarketPlace convenience store and deli and owner's private ski lockers in addition to heated underground valet parking, daily maid service and concierge.

Above and right: The par 3, 207 yard 17th hole at Edgewood Tahoe Golf Course.

Heavenly® Ski Resort's new gondola is literally just outside the door of both Marriott Grand Residence Club and Marriott's Timber Lodge. This is an alpine experience second to none with a 10,067 foot mountain complete with 84 different runs and

service cafeteria, and the Sky Deck with chicken sandwiches and burgers.

"Lake Tahoe... the fairest picture the whole Earth affords."
Mark Twain

For the latest in equipment the resort

nephew Tom Fazio making a number of course improvements over the past decade. Edgewood has hosted many events including the U.S. Senior Open in 1985, the U.S. Public Links Championship in 1980, the A.J.G.A.'s Lake Tahoe Classic and the American Century Celebrity Golf Championship since 1991. The 18 hole championship layout plays at 7,445 yards from the gold tees and down to a gentler 5,567 yards from the red tees.

The Edgewood Restaurant, located in the clubhouse, is a spectacular setting

29 lifts over 4,800 skiable acres in both California and Nevada. The new 138 cabin Gondola is among the fastest in North America. Traveling from the heart of Lake Tahoe to the heart of the mountain in one of the eight passenger cabins takes less than 15 minutes. On the way up passengers travel through trees and straight up the mountain enjoying a spectacular view of the Sierra Nevada.

With an annual snowfall averaging more than 30 feet a year and sunny days averaging an astonishing 76%... days with less than perfect ski conditions are rare. Heavenly® offers seven on-mountain lodges situated in convenient locations around the resort. The lodges include California Lodge, which features a massive 45 item salad bar and a full

offers Heavenly® Sports for skiers and The Boardinghouse for snowboarders. A day care center and skiing and snowboarding lessons are also offered.

with breathtaking views of Lake Tahoe day or night, in any season.

Above left: The beach club provides a tranquil setting for enjoying a day at the lake.

ROBINSON RANCH

Preserving the Grand Traditions of the Early California Ranches

Located in Santa Clarita, just 25 miles north of Los Angeles, Robinson Ranch Golf Club is nestled against the backdrop of the Angeles National Forest. Developed on an early California cattle ranch with gently rolling hills, hundreds of majestic oak trees, towering sycamores and a variety of flowering sage, Robinson Ranch is a collaboration between famed golf course architect Ted Robinson, Sr. and his son Ted, Jr. and features two 18 hole championship golf courses– the Mountain Course, which plays at 6,508 yards and the Valley Course which comes in at 6,903 yards. The club's two golf courses are crafted over 400 acres of mountains, valleys and canyons and are on par with any world-class private club but are open to the public on a daily fee basis.

The Robinsons designed Robinson Ranch with preservation of the natural rolling terrain and hundreds of century old oak trees at the forefront of their plans. Of the project's 400 acres, only 180 were seeded for turf. During the construction process extreme caution was taken to preserve the natural environment including boxing and moving native trees and plants, hand digging irrigation lines and leading bulldozers on foot during grading.

Above: The par 3, 204 yard 6th hole on the Mountain Course, one of the few flat holes on the tract, plays across a lake to a green protected in front by a large bunker.

Left: A mature oak tree in the middle of the fairway on the par 4, 366 yard 12th hole on the Valley Course makes an interesting hazard.

Right: The par 4, 407 yard 16th hole on the Valley Course is bordered to the left and rear by wildflowers while a strategically placed sand bunker and a pristine lake await the errant shot to the right.

The result of these measures, and countless other precautions taken throughout the construction process, was an environmentally friendly golf course that lives in harmony with the ranch's natural terrain. Robinson Ranch is California's first *Audubon Silver Signature Sanctuary* golf facility, an august achievement the Robinson's take very seriously and with pride.

The Mountain Course was the first 18 holes built, opening in December of 1999 and, while the shorter of the two layouts at 6,508 yards, offers terrific shot value over its rolling terrain. The course plays through stands of oaks, native plants and grasses and features dramatic changes in elevation with spectacular views of the Santa Clarita Valley. The area north of the course will never be developed so there will always be a natural feeling. With the course bordering the Angeles National Forest a variety of wildlife can be observed including coyote, deer, bobcat and bear.

Below: The green on the par 4, 283 yard 8th hole on the Valley Course is protected at the front by a series of bunkers and bordered on the left and rear by the Angeles National Forest.

The Valley Course plays nearly 400 yards longer than the Mountain Course, at 6,903 yards from the back tees, making it the more challenging of the two. The course is carved thru the Ranch's natural valley habitats. It is here the Robinson's signature water features come into play on many of the holes including waterfalls and lakes on the 9th and 18th greens. The Valley Course, as well as the Mountain Course, feature the highest quality in putting surfaces with A-4 bent grass greens which are extremely rare for Southern California golf courses. Both the Valley and the Mountain courses provide a fair test of skill for players at any level of the game.

The Robinson Ranch Golf Club's 26,000-square foot clubhouse provides state-

of-the-art facilities and inspiring views of the Angeles National Forest to the north and the returning 18th hole and 9th hole of the Valley Course.

Above: The 26,000-sq. ft. clubhouse overlooks the greens of the 9th hole and 18th hole on the Valley Course.

Far left: The par 4, 402 yard 3rd hole on the Mountain Course.

Left: Sunrise on the par 5, 522 yard 18th hole on the Valley Course.

*Robinson Ranch, an **Audubon Silver Signature Sanctuary** Golf facility, reflects the best attributes of environmentally sound golf courses– natural beauty and memorable golf experiences without destruction of habitat.*

The golf shop is fully equipped to serve players of all handicaps with the finest in equipment and apparel. Tee times are generously staggered to give each golfer plenty of time to enjoy their round and all carts are equipped with an "e-caddy" system electronic range finder.

Before or after your round Robinson Ranch's four-star dining room offers a great selection of delectable entrees in a well appointed setting that can seat up to 300 guests, as well as host social or business events that are planned to perfection by a highly trained PGA professional staff. The clubhouse also offers a conference room with video-conferencing and internet capabilities for up to 30 people.

Robinson Ranch Golf Club offers all the amenities one expects in the finest private country clubs without the long term financial commitments.

Left: The par 3, 171 yard 11th hole on the Valley Course at Robinson Ranch.

135

HILTON
WAIKOLOA VILLAGE

More Hawaiian than You Can Imagine...

O n the Big Island of Hawaii, southernmost in
the chain of Hawaiian Islands, the first daring
Polynesians pulled their rugged dugouts ashore
after crossing 2,000 miles of vast Pacific Ocean.
Here, they settled in the shadow of active volcanoes where
today the fertile land yields rich harvests of macadamia
nuts, sun-ripened papayas and Kona coffee.

The Big Island is a treasure trove of striking contrasts–
tropical beaches and snow-capped mountains, ancient
petroglyphs and modern luxury resorts, like the lavish
Hilton Waikoloa Village. Full of secrets and surprises, this
outstanding property on the Kohala Coast is more Hawaii
than you can imagine, all rolled into one adventure-filled
tropical destination.

Above: Aerial view of the Hilton Waikoloa Village and
the Beach Golf Club.

Right: Hilton Waikoloa Village's natural seawater lagoon
is the ideal snorkeling spot for glimpses of green sea
turtles and schools of colorful topical fish.

The Resort's mile-long Museum Walk provides a leisurely stroll along pink flagstone walkways flanked by tropical gardens and magnificent examples of Polynesian and Oriental artwork.

Guests arriving at Hilton Waikoloa Village can begin their adventure with a relaxing ride in a mahogany canal boat, winding along languid waterways to their spacious accommodations in one of three low-rise towers. If they prefer, guests can travel by air-conditioned tram, whisking past natural lagoons,

waterfalls and hidden tropical grottos. The resort's 1,240 guestrooms and suites in the Lagoon, Palace and Ocean towers are filled with exotic art and antiques; each has a private lanai from which to enjoy tropical breezes and beautiful ocean, golf course or mountain views.

The nine restaurants of Hilton Waikoloa Village are as varied and unique as the Hawaiian Islands

each restaurant offers distinct culinary discoveries and impeccable service.

The ocean waters of Waiulua Bay flow naturally to the sands of Hilton Waikoloa's unique Lagoon Beach. One end of this protected salt-water lagoon is the site of Dolphin Quest, an incredible program operated by marine mammal specialists who are committed to the conservation of dolphins and the marine ecosystem. In the waters of this crystal-clear lagoon, a small group of bottlenose dolphins cavorts in the sandy shallows and interacts with visitors in an educational encounter unlike any other. So popular is this hands-on program that encounters may be booked up to 60 days in advance online at dolphinquest.org.

But dolphins are just one of the amazing attractions at Hilton Waikoloa Village. The

themselves. From casual outdoor dining at Orchid Cafe to the elegance of a traditional Japanese meal at Imari's,

Above: One of three pools at Hilton Waikoloa Village. Left: The water wonderland features pools, waterfalls and a giant water slide.

resort's mile-long Museum Walk is a leisurely stroll along pink flagstone walkways flanked by tropical gardens, waterways filled with brilliant tropical fish and magnificent examples of Polynesian and Oriental artwork.

Three expansive pools located on the grounds invite relaxation and swimming featuring waterfalls, a giant water slide and even a lazy current in the Kohala River Pool. And the European-style Kohala Spa, with its wide range of services, is dedicated to the Hawaiian ideal of harmony between body and spirit for total well being.

Above: Lush tropical landscaping and waterways comprise the 62 acre oceanfront Hilton Waikoloa Village.

Left: Dolphin Quest, an educational encounter unlike any other, allows guests an opportunity to experience dolphins in their natural habitat.

Right: Guest arriving at Hilton Waikoloa Village can begin their adventure with a relaxing ride in a mahogany canal boat along the resort's waterways, which are filled with tropical fish.

Hilton Waikoloa Village is a water wonderland, where guests snorkeling in the resort's four-acre lagoon may spot rare green sea turtles or schools of tropical fish. The hotel's watersport specialists offer deep-water adventure on their 50-foot luxury catamaran. Snorkel sails, scuba diving, whale watch cruises or a romantic evening champagne sail are some of the options available. Nearby Kailua-Kona is the deep-sea fishing capital of the world where anglers regularly battle billfish and blue marlin.

There's no better way to explore the ranchlands that surround Hilton Waikoloa Village than on horseback. Riders can discover cinder cones and ancient Hawaiian ruins.

Carved into the jagged lava fields and flowing alongside the ocean are two championship golf courses at the adjacent Waikoloa Golf Club. The Beach Course is a design of dramatic contrast, a stunning transition from black lava to deep-green golf course. The Kings' Course was a collaboration

of Tom Weiskopf and Jay Morrish, who created a delicate balance between challenge and visual beauty in this links-style layout. In its first full year of operation, the Kings' Course was voted runner-up for "Best New Resort Course in America" by *Golf Digest*.

On this ever-changing island, where Kilauea continues to send molten lava pouring into the sea, one thing is certain... Hilton Waikoloa Village is more Hawaii than one could ever hope for.

Above: Spectacular views from the par 5, 582 yard 12th hole on the Beach Course may include Humpback whales.

Far left: *Hanalei*, this beautiful statue graces the 12th green on the Ocean Course.

Left: A view of the salt-water lagoon.

LOST CANYONS GOLF CLUB

Links-Style Layouts in California's Santa Susana Mountain Range...

Lost Canyons Golf Club, LA's newest destination resort, is a high-end daily fee facility featuring 36 holes of championship golf designed by world-renown golf course architect Pete Dye with golf course consultant Fred Couples for Landmark National. Pete Dye has designed some of the most legendary and recognizable golf courses in the world including five on *Golf Magazine's* Top 100 Courses in the World– Casa de Campo in La Romana, Dominican Republic; The Golf Club in New Albany, Ohio; Whistling Straits in Haven, Wisconsin; TPC at Sawgrass in Ponte Vedra Beach, Florida and The Honors Course in Ooltewah, Tennessee. Dye, well known for creating some of golf's more memorable challenges, has earned a reputation for an ever-present emphasis on environmental protection.

Left: The par 4, 485 yard , 9th hole, *Sky Lake,* on the Sky Course requires a well placed tee shot to carry the lake and a fairway bunker and an accurate second shot to avoid bunkers on the right and left sides of the green.

Above: The par 3, 205 yard 16th hole, *Scout,* on the Shadow Course presents a target green. Natural areas between the tee and green are environmentally sensitive and are out of bounds.

The collaboration between Pete Dye and PGA Tour great Fred Couples has created a distinctive links layout on the 1,640 acre site in the Simi Valley. Although just 45 minutes north of Los Angeles, Lost Canyons feels like you are worlds away from the hustle and bustle of the city. There are few distractions here.

The Sky Course was selected by *Golf Magazine* as one of the **Top 10 Best New Courses in 2001** and the Shadow Course earned honors as one of the **Top 10 Best New Courses in 2002**.

The Sky Course follows canyon ridge lines offering spectacular panoramic views while the Shadow Course winds along the rolling canyon floor and affords breathtaking views of White Face Mountain. Both golf courses place

premiums on accuracy and positioning. With five sets of tees, one has only to select their comfort level to enjoy a truly unique golf experience.

The Sky Course features back-to-back par-5s on the 4th and 5th holes that cover 1140 yards and a par-4, 9th hole that is 485 yards from the back tees. The par-5, 12th and 14th holes exceed 600 yards each while the par-3, 17th looks 30 miles past the hanging green to the Los Angeles National Forest.

"The views are unbelievable. There are times that you look around and think that you are in Montana."

Fred Couples

Above: *Lookout Point*, the par 4, 460 yard 18th hole on the Sky Course.

Far left: *Trail Head*, the par 4, 310 yard 1st hole on the Shadow Course.

Left: *Hawk's Bluff*, the par 3, 170 yard 17th hole on the Sky Course.

The Shadow Course, set on lower ground than the Sky Course, flows through the natural terrain of Dry Creek Canyon below the Santa Susana Mountains. Box canyons and shadows cast by canyon walls create an intimate feeling. Reminiscent of the Old Course at St. Andrews, the Shadow Course plays through rolling fairways and trench-like bunkers to its farthest point at the 9th hole before making the turn for the clubhouse. Less grading was necessary on the Shadow Course than the Sky Course resulting in a less forgiving layout.

Lost Canyons 20,000 square-foot club house features a fully-appointed golf shop and dining room with indoor and outdoor seating for tournaments and group outings of any size. The practice facilities, golf academy and optional

professionally-trained forecaddies offer a level of service normally only found only in the finest private clubs.

Landmark National has developed more than 25 golf courses including PGA West, Mission Hills, Carmel Valley Ranch and Kiawah Island. Landmark's experience guarantees Lost Canyons will be fondly remembered long after the last putt has dropped.

Above: The Sky Course's 615 yard 12th hole, *Devil's Slide*, is named for a part of the old Wells Fargo stage line through the Santa Susana Mountains that was so steep passengers got out and walked down the hill.

Right: *Scout*, the par 3, 205 yard 16th hole on the Shadow Course plays across Dry Creek.

"This is the most majestic piece of property I've ever had to work with, nothing else comes close. The long views and topography here are just spectacular"

Pete Dye

Far left: The par 4, 335 yard 13th hole on the Shadow Course, *Cougar Den,* requires a well-placed tee shot to clear the pot bunker in the center of the fairway to leave an uphill pitch to the green (left) which is a sharp dogleg right.

MARRIOTT'S
CANYON VILLAS

The Sonoran Desert Blends Effortlessly with World-Class Golf at Desert Ridge...

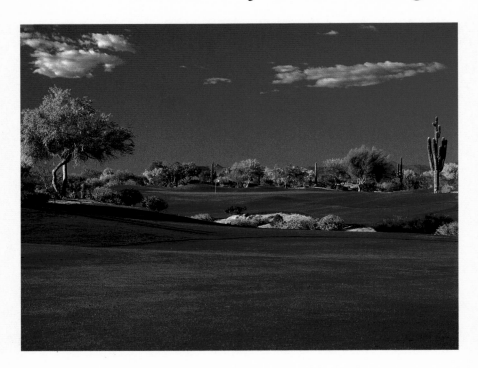

An oasis surrounded by the pristine Sonoran Desert in the heart of the Valley of the Sun where Phoenix meets Scottsdale, Marriott's Canyon Villas at Desert Ridge® is poised to capture the best of resort living. With two championship golf courses and a wealth of outdoor activities including horseback riding, hot-air ballooning, off-road excursions and hiking nearby, Desert Ridge® offers the active vacationer a world of excitement. Full use of shared resort amenities with the adjacent JW Marriott Desert Ridge® Resort and Spa, the largest luxury resort in Arizona, adds four acres of waterways for swimming; an adult lap pool; a feature pool with waterfall and fire show and a lazy river with a water slide; a children's activity center; a tennis pavilion with grass and clay courts; a world-class fitness center; a two-level 28,000-square foot spa with 41 treatment rooms, and nine exciting dining venues including Roy's Pacific Rim and Blue Sage by Mark Miller to the mix.

Above: The par 4, 450 yard 2nd hole on the Arnold Palmer Course.

Right: The par 3, 220 yard 7th hole on the Faldo Course is completely guarded on the left by an elaborately sculpted sand bunker.

At Canyon Villas, Wildfire® Golf Club offers a dynamic golf experience with two championship courses, including 18 holes of Nick Faldo challenges and 18 holes of Arnold Palmer's undulating greens to test your skills. The Faldo Course plays at 6,846 yards from the tournament tees and 5,245 yards from the forward tees while The Arnold Palmer Signature Course plays at 7,145 yards from the tournament tees and 5,505 from the forward tees.

The two 18-hole layouts at Marriott's Desert Ridge® have distinct characteristics, yet each shares the incredible Sonoran Desert landscape, views of the McDowell Mountains to the east and sweeping views of Mummy Mountain and Camelback Mountain to the south. The Faldo Course sits on a 174 acre site with generous fairways, large bent grass greens and tees and some 106 well-sculpted sand bunkers, some lining an entire fairway. The bunkers are well placed and allow

allows the individual player to select a tee that meets their individual skill level, creating a fair test for the lower handicap golfers and an enjoyable outing for the higher handicap player.

The Palmer Course plays nearly 300 yards longer than the Faldo Course and offers strategic hazards as it integrates the Sonoran Desert seamlessly throughout the golf course. Lush with exotic blooming cacti, mesquite, palo verde trees and wild sage, the course is very playable with expansive fairways, flashed bunkering and large putting greens (averaging 7,000-square feet) creating a delightful balance between challenge and visual beauty.

players to determine the amount of challenge they wish to face and offer an opportunity to use a variety of shot making skills. The course's multiple tee placements also

The state-of-the-art practice facilities at Wildfire® Golf Club include an all grass driving range with grass tees, putting and chipping greens, and a fairway bunker. The 25,000-square foot masterfully designed clubhouse is highlighted by the Steakhouse at Wildfire® Golf Club's restaurant and bar, an extensive golf shop and dramatic

views of the McDowell Mountains. The golf shop carries the latest and highest quality golf apparel, accessories and a range of equipment choices.

Top left: The par 3, 160 yard 5th hole on the Arnold Palmer Signature Course. Top Right: The par 5, 534 yard 9th hole on the Faldo Course. Above: The par 4, 341 yard 8th hole on the Faldo Course is guarded on the right by a sand bunker more than 180 yards long. Left: The par 4, 408 yard 2nd hole on the Faldo Course.

M arriott's Canyon Villas are located within the Desert Ridge® community. The planned 252 two-bedroom, two-bath villas are arranged in intimate settings around courtyards along the golf course and throughout the Sonoran Desert on the resort's 22 acre landscaped grounds. Each of the villa's enjoy perfectly placed private decks or patios overlooking either the Wildfire® golf course or the spectacular Sonoran Desert. In addition to sharing the amenities of the adjacent JW Marriott Desert Ridge® Resort and Spa, Marriott's Canyon Villas offers many on site amenities including a courtyard pool that includes a children's pool, two whirlpool spas and a pool bar. There's even a fire pit designed as a focal point for evening social gatherings.

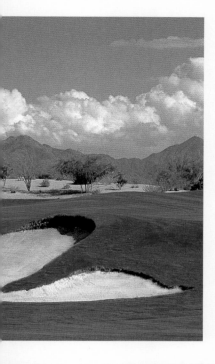

Each of the distinctly designed and tastefully appointed 1,260-square foot two bedroom, two bathroom Canyon Villas can accommodate as many as eight people in comfort.

The luxurious master suite offers a king-size bed, television, an oversized soaking tub, vanity and a separate shower with its own vanity. The villa's guest suite features a full bath, king-size bed, a double sleeper sofa in the sitting area, television, its own entrance and a private balcony or patio furnished with outdoor furniture.

The spacious living area provides a queen-size sleeper sofa, an entertainment center with a television and a video cassette player and access to the balcony. The villa's dining area accommodates six comfortably with a breakfast bar that provides seating for two.

The Canyon Villa's deluxe kitchen is fully equipped with dishwasher, oven, microwave, full size refrigerator, and dinnerware service for eight. Other Villa amenities include a utility room with a washer and dryer and linens for eight.

Where the fairway's edge meets the desert the scent of sage prevails in an environment of stately saguaros, flowering ocotillo, beavertail, cholla and barrel cacti that is home to cottontail and jackrabbit, coyote, javelina, red-tailed hawk, roadrunners, chuckwalla and Gambel quail. It's a scenic wonderland in which to enjoy bicycling and hiking. The adjacent 110-acre Desert Ridge® Marketplace offers a variety of entertainment, dining and retail choices.

Marriott's Canyon Villas are available through Marriott Vacation Club International which offers a variety of ownership options and features.

Top left: The par 4, 460 yard 10th hole on the Faldo Course is protected at the front by a series of sculpted bunkers.

Above: The par 4, 360 yard 13th hole on the Faldo Course features a large sand bunker with native desert vegetation planted in its center.

Left: A view across the green on the Faldo Course's par 3, 214 yard, 14th hole to the McDowell Mountains in the background.

"Top Twenty U.S. Courses."
Golfweek

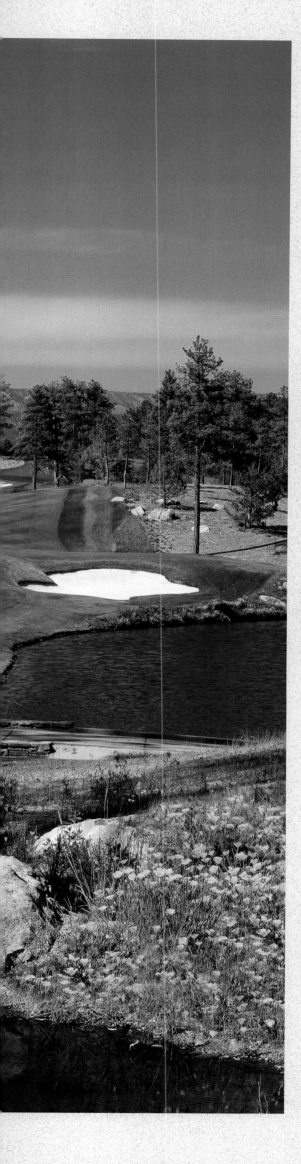

THE RIM GOLF CLUB

Celebrating High Country Living in the Heart of Arizona's Mogollon Rim Country.

Nestled among the largest contiguous stand of Ponderosa pine in North America, The Rim Golf Club resides in a truly unique setting rich with the natural beauty of Arizona's Mogollon Rim country. Created for those who not only hold nature in high regard but who want to participate in its splendor, The Rim Golf Club is Arizona's ultimate residential mountain golf community. Serene, picturesque and recognized for excellence in design, the Tom Weiskopf and Jay Morrish designed course has quickly risen to its destined place among the country's finest with a recent ranking in the **Top 20 U.S. Golf Courses** by *Golfweek*, the highest ranking of any Arizona golf course.

Payson, Arizona's mild temperatures year-round keeps The Rim Golf Club course open for play in all seasons. And with a membership that is restricted to just 295 equity members, there's peace and solitude on most days.

Above: The 431 yard, par 4, 16th hole, *Monument Valley*, framed against a backdrop of Arizona's majestic Mogollon Rim.

Left: *Genus Loci*, the par 5, 533 yard 9th hole, plays downhill and with the prevailing wind to shorten it just a bit. The Rim Golf Club's 5,000 foot elevation adds about 8% to each club's length.

"I personally feel that holes 7 through 18 at The Rim Golf Club are the finest consecutive holes that Jay and I have ever designed."

Tom Weiskopf

The Rim Club is well situated for a primary residence or a family retreat. The easy drive north from Phoenix along Highway 87 winds through some of the most picturesque scenery found anywhere in Arizona. At just over an hour from the metropolitan area, The Rim Golf Club is close enough for convenience, yet far enough to be a world of its own.

A temperate climate at an elevation of 5,000 feet gives The Rim Golf Club the best of each season: idyllic spring days with 60-70 degree temperatures; summer with nighttime lows some twenty-five degrees cooler than those of the desert regions below the Rim; a fall with just a hint of briskness and splashes of showy color, and winters with occasional dustings of snow.

Pine-covered mountains, clear lakes and streams, and forest trails provide endless recreational opportunities for outdoor enthusiasts to hike, camp,

horseback ride, hunt, fish, bird-watch, boat, water ski, swim or just relax and enjoy the natural beauty of the Tonto National Forest, the second largest in the United States. With more than 580,000 acres of riparian habitat— biotic communities along banks of streams, rivers and lakes— the forest's diversity supports an abundance of flora and fauna. In these regions, explorers can experience the virgin forest in all its grandeur, and in solitude.

Above to the right: *Genus Loci*, the par 5, 533 yard, 9th hole plays to an elevated green. To the left, *Elk Trail*, the par 4, 455 yard, 10th hole has a downhill tee shot and an uphill second shot into the prevailing wind.

The Rim Golf Club's Tom Weiskopf and Jay Morrish designed golf course, one of their last collaborations, takes every advantage of the landscape to deliver a challenging and awe-inspiring round of golf. The club's limited membership allows members to enjoy the game in its purest form. There are no assigned tee times and the practice facilities are said to be the finest Tom and Jay have ever created.

Carved from the Ponderosa pine and junipers, fairways stretch to 400 feet wide. The soft rolls of the fairway transition effortlessly into the surrounding forest. Expansive views framed by the Stewart Mountains from the south and the seemingly endless stretch of the Mogollon Rim to the north, the sparkle of clear blue lakes, oversized greens make a round at The Rim Golf Club a visual pleasure.

To preserve the pristine forest setting, fifty percent of the land area of The Rim Golf Club is to remain in its natural state. Homesites are carefully located to capture the natural forest setting and to preserve the environment.

Estate homesites, averaging 1.2 acres each, are situated on hillsides above tree-lined fairways to capture views of the course and surrounding mountains while half-acre Golf Club homesites are nestled in the shade of towering pines.

The Rim Golf Club is part of the Crescent Resources, L.L.C. real estate development group.

Above: A white-tailed deer in velvet. The diverse habitat of the Tonto National Forest, the second largest in the United States, is home to varied flora and fauna.

Right: *Pine Stream*, the par 4, 467 yard 7th hole, plays downhill to a large green.

Formed more than 30 years ago by Duke Energy, the company has land interests in eight states in the Southeast and Southwest.

The unique setting of The Rim Golf Club is still attainable.

Far left: *Boulder to Boulder,* the par 4, 435 yard 14th hole. The Mogollon Rim, a mountainous plateau with a 7,000 foot elevation that extends for some 200 miles, can be seen in the distance.

Left: *Spirit Hollow,* the par 5, 581 yard, 13th hole is framed by a massive boulder outcropping reaching seven-stories high.

LANDMARK GOLF CLUB

The Home of The Skins Game...

ocated in the foothills of Indio, California, Landmark Golf Club, consists of two championship 18 hole golf courses set among hundreds of acres of natural terrain. The golf club was designed as a venue for professional golf events by Landmark Golf Company and golf course designers Schmidt-Curley Design to promote the spirit and competition of the game of golf. The two courses, the Skins North Course and the Skins South Course, play through a variety of unique landforms, steep slopes, three refreshing lakes, different soil types, rolling sand dunes and natural desert flora. The Skins North Course plays 7,123 yards from the tournament tees and 5,015 yards from the forward tees while the Skins South course ranges from 7,229 yards at the tournament tees to 5,094 yards from the forward tees. The Skins North Course rating is 74.3 with a slope of 135. The Skins South Course rating is 75.1 with a slope of 136.

Above: *Options*, the par 4, 373 yard 12th hole on the Skins North Course.

Right: A view from the tees on the dogleg right, par 4, 334 yard 14th hole on the Skins North Course to the green, which is surrounded by bunkers on front, right and left and by water to the left, right and back.

The Skins courses are studies in contrast in textures and colors as they roll perfectly maintained emerald green tees, fairways and greens through colorful native desert vegetation. Landmark's signature bridges are crafted from vintage railroad cars, an interesting side bar to the day's round. Adding to the natural beauty of the golf courses and surrounding mountains are magnificent sunrises and sunsets as the entire Coachella Valley provides a backdrop.

Landmark Golf Club has been the home of the Skins Game since 1999. The annual made for television event takes place on Thanksgiving weekend and consists each year of four of golf's strongest competitors. The tournament takes advantage of both courses by playing on nine holes of the Skins North Course and nine holes of the Skins South over two days. The golfers battle for the $1,000,000 purse with the first six holes being worth $25,000 each, the second six holes are worth $50,000 each, holes 13 through 17 are

worth $70,000 each and the 18th is worth $200,000. The foursome plays for $300,000 on Saturday and $700,000 on Sunday. Each of the four players in the tournament must agree to donate 20% of their winnings, $200,000 from the $1,000,000 purse, to their favorite charities. The tournaments $1,000,000 purse makes it one of the richest two-day events in the game of golf.

Far left: The par 4, 405 yard 10th hole on the Skins South Course.

Left: The par 3, 183 yard 15th hole on the Skins North Course is all carry.

Below: Greg Norman blast his way from a bunker on the par 4, 408 yard 16th hole.

The Landmark Golf Academy staff offers students the tools necessary to elevate their game to a new level. Students can choose from individual lessons or one of the academy's programs. Lesson options include playing lessons, corporate/group lessons, a junior program, private instruction and family instruction. Golf tournaments of any size can also be accommodated at the club.

For dining and banquet facilities Landmark Golf Club offers the clubhouse with a dining room that overlooks the large lake where the 14th, 15th and 18th greens converge together and features a traditional country club fare but will customize a menu for any occasion. Also offered are the "Skins Pavilion," which can accommodate groups of up to 250 people for special events, beverage carts and

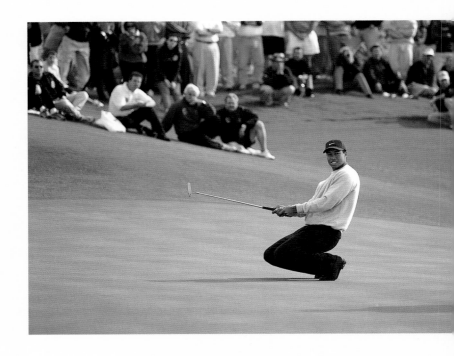

halfway houses. Additional services offered include valet parking, bag storage and Callaway rental clubs.

Landmark Golf Club was developed by Landmark Golf Company/ Schmidt-Curley Design whose principals developed such recognizable golf properties as PGA West, Carmel Valley Ranch, Oak Tree Golf Club, La Quinta Hotel Golf & Tennis Resort and Kiawah Island among others.

Far left: Tiger Woods at the 2001 Skins Game. The Skins Game offers an opportunity to be up close and personal with the players.

Left: A side view of *Star Wars,* the par 3, 192 yard 12th hole on the Skins South Course.

Below: The 1st hole on the Skins South Course, *Rocky Peak*, is a 382 yard par 4 surrounded by the natural desert.

"Top Ten You Can Play."
Golf Magazine

RANCHO SAN MARCOS

Established in 1804, Rancho San Marcos is a Unique Part of Santa Barbara's Past...

Tucked within a valley floor in the Santa Ynez Mountains, Rancho San Marcos Golf Course offers a unique opportunity to play a round through terrain featuring centuries old California oak trees and the workings of the historic Rancho San Marcos. The 6,800 yard par-71 course was designed by Robert Trent Jones, Jr. to preserve the natural beauty of the land. Magnificent vistas await at every turn over 300 spectacular acres that create an interesting challenge to golfers of all abilities while not intruding on the environment and natural habitat for a variety of wildlife. With no trace of urban development, Rancho San Marcos is the ideal location to forget your worldly cares and enjoy the peaceful solitude of a bygone era.

Rancho San Marcos features several unique amenities including sandstone wood burning fireplaces placed around the course for chilly mornings, baskets of fresh fruit await at several tees and there is even an original 1860 stagecoach trail used for the cart path along the 17th fairway. In May of 2000 *Golf Digest* listed Rancho San Marcos among the **Top 201 Places to Play in North America** for outstanding achievement in customer service and course conditioning.

Above: Original Rancho San Marcos Ranch buildings serve as the golf shop, cart barn and offices overlooking the practice putting green.

Left: *Figueroa*, the par 3, 203 yard 5th hole, is guarded by a pristine lake that, in addition to adding an element of risk for an errant shot, is popular with local wildlife and migrating waterfowl.

Rancho San Marcos has all the amenities normally associated with only the finest private clubs including a practice facility with all grass tees, chipping and putting areas, and unlimited range balls stacked in pyramids. If you decide to walk professionally trained caddies will carry your clubs, note yardages and assist you with the nuances of the course.

Expert instruction with advanced video training is available and golf clinics and schools may be arranged for groups that range from half-day sessions to three-day golf schools custom tailored for all players' abilities and facets of the game. Classes are designed with low student-to-instructor ratios to insure quality attention and instruction needed to help shape and improve your skills. The well appointed golf shop offers the latest in equipment, apparel and accessories from the leading names in golf.

Davy Stable Cafe serves breakfast and lunch from a delicious menu using only the freshest ingredients prepared to order. Golfers can dine in a wonderfully intimate atmosphere, sit on the patio overlooking the lake and golf course, or take out. Rancho San Marcos also features an on-course refreshment service with a variety of beverages, delectables and cold towels.

Rancho San Marcos is just 15 minutes west of Santa Barbara's beaches and 15 minutes east of the wine country community of Santa Ynez and the Danish themed village of Solvang.

Above: *Davy Stables*, the par 4, 404 yard 9th hole, is guarded along the left by a lake and to the right by a series of sculpted bunkers.

Right: *Eagle's Nest*, the par 3, 175 yard 14th hole, plays across an arroyo to a gently sloping green.

Far left: *Los Padres*, the par 5, 542 yard 18th hole, is well protected by a large bunker at the left front and a series of sculpted bunkers on the right and to the rear.

Left: *San Fernando*, the par 3, 223 yard, 16th hole is guarded by a massive bunker system that starts in front of the green and continues all along its right side.

RAVEN GOLF CLUB
AT SOUTH MOUNTAIN

A Traditional Layout in the Heart of the Sonoran Desert...

Above: The 324 yard, par 4, 5th hole requires an accurate second shot to escape the well bunkered apron.

Above right: The par 5, 526 yard 9th hole has its own tranquil setting surrounded by a pine forest.

Left: The par 3, 14th hole plays between 123 and 167 yards.

A Midwestern treasure in the heart of the Valley of the Sun, the Raven Golf Club at South Mountain has distinguished itself since its inception in 1995 as one of Arizona's premier golf experiences. This upscale daily fee course, designed by former US Open and PGA Championship winner David Graham and award-winning golf course architect Gary Panks, features a 7,078 yard layout. Plush, rolling fairways are framed by more than six thousand mature Aleppo, Mondale and Canary Island pines along with African Sumac and oleander as well as vistas of rugged desert mountains and the Phoenix skyline. Combining great design, meticulous conditions and outstanding guest service, the Raven at South Mountain creates the ambiance and feel of a private country club and lasting memories for those fortunate enough to play a round.

"From day one, when Gary and I began to layout the Raven at South Mountain, I knew we had something very special."

David Graham

The Raven at South Mountain's pine forest sets the stage for a traditional Midwestern golf experience, which may at first seem a little out of place in its desert setting, but has become a welcome departure from the Valley of the Sun's plethora of desert courses. Here, emphasis is on the quality of the golf experience and service, evidenced by praise from the golf community including honors as "#1 in Golf Course Service

in North America" by *Golf Digest*. The Raven's staff enjoys a reputation reflecting attention to detail in course conditions and the highest quality in guest service.

David Graham and Gary Panks were able to transform the foothills of Phoenix's South Mountain into a layout that challenges skilled veterans of the game, yet at the same time remains enjoyable for average players. The 7,078 yard golf course features

beautiful beds of Georgia pine mulch separating in bounds and out-of-play areas and countless flower gardens accenting the greens and tees. Vistas of the rugged desert mountains or the Phoenix skyline await at every hole, with sunsets adding a special glow at the end of the day.

The three most challenging holes the Raven at South Mountain offers are the par 4, 477 yard, 3rd hole, a lot of golf between tee and green to make par; the 593 yard, par 5, 17th hole which plays even longer with a pair of fairway bunkers guarding the right side on the second shot; and the 596 yard, par 5, 4th hole, with the right front and side of the green protected by a giant bunker.

Birdie attempts are most likely on the 167 yard, par 3, 14th hole; the 137 yard, par 3, 2nd hole; the 195 yard, par 3, 11th hole and the 325 yard, par 4, 5th hole.

Above: The par 4, 453 yard, 16th hole sets the stage for a strong trio of finishing holes, each a true test of shot-making skills.

The Raven Golf Club at South Mountain is the perfect site for tournaments and group outings, providing all the necessary ingredients to ensure memorable events. From the dramatic challenge of the golf course to the comfort of the hacienda-style clubhouse, guests enjoy a golf experience and personal service without equal in a public golf course.

Owned and managed by Intrawest Golf of Scottsdale, Arizona, the Raven Golf Clubs are synonymous with excellence. More than just a symbol or a logo, the Raven is a commitment to provide discerning players high-quality golf experiences unique to their environments with superior course conditioning and outstanding guest service. Along with the Raven at Three Peaks (Silverthorne, Colorado), the Raven at

Sandestin (Destin, Florida) and the Raven at Snowshoe Mountain (Snowshoe, West Virginia), the Raven Golf Club at South Mountain is dedicated to providing its guests with indelible memories.

Above: The ponds and lakes at 18th green have become a haven for migrating waterfowl.

Right: An expansive bunker, shared by the 2nd and 4th holes, collects any errant shots right of the green on the par 5, 4th hole. The hole's 596 yard length makes it a challenge for distance.

Above right: The hacienda-style clubhouse features a full service golf shop and sports club dining.

Left: An elaborate water hazard comes into play on the right side in front of the green and wraps around the right and the back of the green on the par 4, 428 yard, 18th hole. The safest approach is from the left side of the fairway.

THE FIJI ISLANDS

The Fijian People Extend a Warm Greeting of "Bula"...

Scattered amid the balmy waters of the South Pacific are the more than 300 coral isles which comprise the Fiji archipelago... home to a gracious, dignified people whose rich culture reflects a living tradition of sincere hospitality. The Fijian people are considered their country's greatest natural resource, as visitors to the islands from around the globe soon discover. Once guest are greeted with a warm smile and a heartfelt "bula," which literally translates as "good health" and is used to say *hello, goodbye, thank you* and *I will miss you,"* they know they've arrived for the most unique, refreshing adventure imaginable.

Living is good in the Fiji Islands. Uncrowded and unspoiled, this cluster of islands is packed with unique experiences; coral reefs, mangrove forests and natural limestone grottos wait to be explored. Scuba diving in Fiji is among the best in the world, with a profusion of tropical fish that live, undisturbed, in the protection of colorful offshore reefs.

Left: An aerial few of a few of the 322 islands that comprise the Fiji Islands archipelago in the South Pacific.

Above: The pool area is beachside at the Sheraton Royal Denarau on the main island of Viti Levu.

Arriving in the Fiji Islands is a pleasure in itself aboard Air Pacific, Fiji's national flag carrier. Air Pacific offers non-stop 747 service from Los Angeles to Fiji's International Airport in Nadi, on the main island of Viti Levu. Air Pacific crew members and service staff are well-versed in the warmth of the Fijian spirit, making every flight a pleasant and hospitable experience.

Upon arrival in Nadi, it's a short jaunt to the international-class resorts of Denarau Island. One of the area's finest is the Sheraton Royal, on the palm-fringed shores of Nadi Bay.

The Sheraton Royal's five-star facilities include beachside accommodations, an intimately landscaped pool area surrounded by coconut palms and tropical plants, three restaurants and not-to-be-missed Fiji-style entertainment including firewalking and "mekes," traditional Fijian songs and dances presented as a living art form.

Guests take advantage of the adjacent 18-hole championship golf course at Denarau Golf & Racquet Club, where sand bunkers and greens take shape in the form of marlin, crab and even a wily octopus. Surrounded by the sea on three sides, the golf course is designed around the island's extensive tidal waterways; pure, natural seawater continually flows into these waterways, enveloping players with the scent of the sea and creating a spectacular water hazard.

Unique and challenging for players at all levels, the layout at Denarau is set among thousands of coconut palms and massive beds of tropical flowers. The open-air design of the Denarau clubhouse is planned around a series of courtyards, leading guests to a restaurant, lounge and complete pro shop. Ten tennis courts, four lighted and six natural grass, round out the club's facilities.

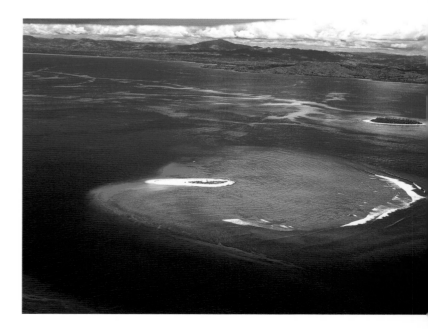

Above: A side view of the seaside 15th green at the Denarau Golf & Racquet Club.

Farthest left: A traditional Fijian sunset torch-lighting ceremony, with wooden drums, on the beach at the Sheraton Royal Denarau.

Far left: The famous surfing and water sport islands of Namotu and Tavarua.

Left: The fairway view to the green of the par 4, 402 meter, 15th hole.

VATULELE
ISLAND RESORT

The ultimate in private resort living is found on the romantic isle of Vatulele (*Vah-too-lay-lay*), at the exquisite Vatulele Island Resort. Situated 30 miles off the Coral Coast of Viti Levu, Vatulele is a 12-square-mile island shaped something like a footprint in the sand. A coral reef completely embraces the limestone island, creating a protective lagoon along the mile-long beach that fronts Vatulele Island Resort. With no other "western" development on the

entire island, it's very hard to imagine a more intimate hideaway than the 16 hand-crafted villas of Vatulele.

Here is a destination for those who think they have seen and had it all. Each of the identical 2,000-square-foot villas, or Fijian "bures" as they are known, is nestled amid coconut palms on its own private stretch of white-sand beach. Natural materials form Vatulele's unique architecture, an intriguing blend of Mediterranean influences with Santa Fe adobe and Fijian thatched roofs. Designed ideally for couples, the bures have spacious sitting rooms, king beds in adjoining raised bedrooms and private terraces with hammocks fronting the beach.

Everything about Vatulele is designed to promote relaxation, warm friendships and a general sense of well-being. There are no monetary transactions on the island, nor are there telephones, newspapers or television. All meals, beverages and activities are included

in the room tariff, and staff members are not permitted to accept individual tips.

The food is extraordinary, centered around locally grown fresh produce and seafood and served on an outdoor terrace overlooking the lagoon or, by night, tables are set under the stars and lit by lanterns and candlelight.

Guests will leave Vatulele Island Resort with renewed spirits and a true appreciation for the warmth of the Fijian people, And they'll want to say "vinaka," (thank you), for the genuine graciousness of their Fijian hosts.

Left and above: The float planes in the lagoon and on the beach are used to ferry guests from island to island.

Above left: The entrance to Vatulele Island Resort.

THE MYSTICAL BEAUTY OF BALI

The Island of the Gods...

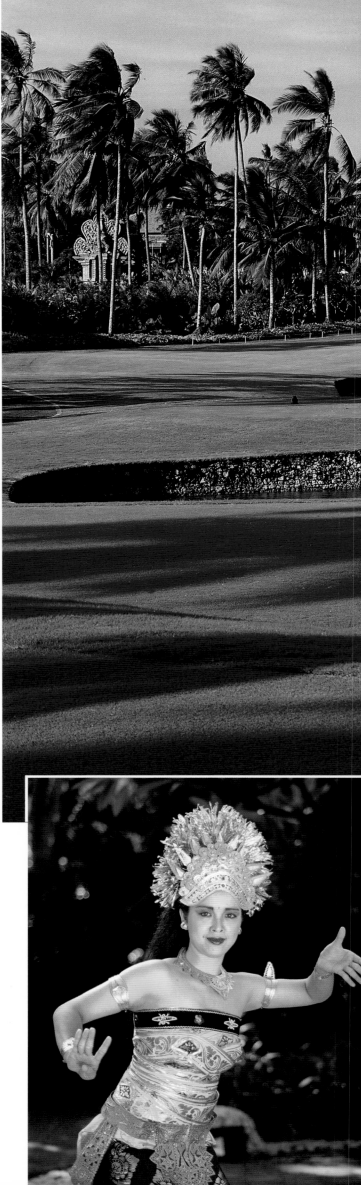

Full of legends and magical tales, the island of Bali is a colorful procession of festivals, music and exotic dances presented by its warm, gentle people. The southernmost end to a string of shimmering islands between Thailand and Australia, Bali is Indonesia's radiant gift to the world, a place of spiritual complexities and innocent charm. Marco Polo came here nearly seven centuries ago looking for spice. Sophisticated travelers arrive on Bali's shores from around the world today, seeking its cultural wonders and tropical climate.

Above: An elaborate Balinese water garden filled with plumeria, water lily and orchids. The carved stone figures spouting water pointing toward the Bali Hindu temple in the background, typify Balinese architecture.

Right: Ancient Balinese dances were almost invariably based on religious belief. The dancers themselves were viewed as a holy-link to the heavens.

Above: The par 3, 160 yard 12th hole at Bali Golf & Country Club. Upon arrival at the 6th and 12th holes golfers are offered cold, rolled linen towels on silver trays by Balinese attendants.

Right: Using a series of interconnecting pools and lagoons, the designers patterned the Grand Hyatt Bali after magnificent island water palaces.

Bali is a land of contrasts, from lush, humid mountains to arid coastal lowlands with fresh, persistent breezes. Terraced rice fields sidestep down the hillsides, and graceful coconut palms sway rhythmically over white sand beaches. At the southern tip of the island is Nusa Dua, Bali's newest beach resort named after twin headlands which jut out into the turquoise sea. Here, the mystical culture of the gentle Balinese people blends in perfect harmony with world-class facilities to create an international enclave of impressive resort hotels.

temple. The people of Bali practice a form of Hinduism dating from the 7th century; many blend both Hindu and

The buildings are designed in traditional island style, with strict adherence to guidelines that no building be taller than the coconut trees and all must contain at least one Balinese

Buddhist principles in a daily ritual of offerings which may be as simple as a spoonful of rice on a delicate leaf tray or as elaborate as tropical floral arrangements and flags.

Estimates suggest there are more than 20,000 Hindu temples in Bali, not counting the small shrines in homes, schools and offices.

Ancient religion of the Balinese even plays a part within Nusa Dua's sunny resort hotels. One elegant resort, the Grand Hyatt Bali, is patterned after the exquisite Balinese water palaces of old. Four ethnic villages are clustered within an interconnecting series of cascading waterfalls, tropical gardens and koi filled lagoons that meander through the resort's 40 acres and on into the sea. The Grand Hyatt Bali enjoys the longest stretch of beachfront in the entire area, and features six pools and a waterslide in an elaborately designed, terraced tropically landscaped water playground.

Each of the hotel's 750 rooms has a distinct Balinese feel. Grass mats cover the floors, furnishings are light, and flowering orchids and hibiscus cascade over patio walls. Grand Hyatt offers five separate dining experiences, with

seafood, Chinese, Italian, Indonesian and Japanese restaurants all located on the property. In evening, intriguing sounds of traditional Balinese instruments accompany the ethnic dancers who perform in the resort's central lobby area. Ancient Balinese dances were almost invariably based on religious belief.

Top far left: The Four Seasons Resort Bali overlooking Jimbaran Bay.

Top left: A reflecting pool greets visitors at the Grand Hyatt Bali with spacious views of the lagoon and gardens extending to the ocean.

Above: Gracefully decorated bamboo poles line the streets of Bali.

Left: A typical Balinese terraced hillside creates the par 3, 175 yard uphill 6th hole at Bali Golf & Country Club.

The game of golf has found its way to Bali and has flourished. Adjacent to the Grand Hyatt Bali is the internationally acclaimed Bali Golf and Country Club, an 18-hole championship course in a spectacular seaside setting. Designed by Robin Nelson and Rodney Wright, the course plays through three distinctly different environments. Holes 1 to 9 travel uphill and provide sweeping views of Nusa Dua, the Indian Ocean and Bali's sacred volcano, Mount Agung. Holes 10 through 16 play along gently sculptured fairways through a mature coconut grove; they're bordered by deeply contoured sand bunkers groomed in artistic patterns. The final two holes run along the beach and face the prevailing winds before winding up at the Balinese-style clubhouse.

As design elements throughout the course, Nelson and Wright incorporated small stone walls reminiscent of rice field terraces to shore up the sides of fairways and tees. Balinese culture also appears through hand carved stone tee markers and intricate stone godlets that serve as the 150-yard markers; there's even an authentic, actively used temple located on the beach just off the 17th hole.

For the ultimate in privacy, the villas of Four Seasons Resort Bali are unsurpassed. Within close proximity to Bali Golf and Country Club, the thatched-roof pavilions of Four Seasons house one- and two-bedroom villas beautifully designed for open air living. The indoor environment becomes a natural extension of the resort's lovely outdoor surroundings, with screened louvered doors and refreshing outdoor showers in secluded gardens.

Each villa has its own private courtyard entered through carved and painted Balinese double doors. Private plunge pools and luxuriant pocket gardens add to the serenity, and the air is fragrant with the scent of frangipani. As a homage to the gods, the Balinese have a small temple within each villa, and offerings of beautifully arranged flowers are made daily.

Scuba diving, white-water rafting, kayaking, hiking and water skiing on the glassy surface of a volcanic lake are available. Shopping for local crafts such including stone and wood carvings, batik prints and ikat cloth is a real treat as well. But the people of Bali are the true lure of this island, with their sacred practices and their complex culture. The warm hospitality and intriguing rituals of the Balinese are sure to stir the soul of all who visit here.

Top left and above: The Balinese style open-sided living pavilion surrounded by traditional courtyard walls at the Four Seasons Resort Bali.

Left: Mature coconut groves and deeply sculptured bunkers are typical of the back nine at Bali Golf & Country Club.

Following pages: Tanah Lot Temple is one of the six most important Bali Hindu temples, attributed to the 16th century priest Dang Hyang Niratha.

DIRECTORY

Bridges at Rancho Santa Fe
6670 Avenida del Daque
Rancho Santa Fe, California 92067
Phone: 858-756-8700
Web site: www.TheBridgesRSF.com

Copper Mountain Resort
104 Wheeler Place
Copper Mountain, Colorado 80443
Phone: 970-968-3333
Web site: www.Intrawestgolf.com
Reservations: (888) 219-2441
Course Designer: Pete & Perry Dye

Cutthroat Anglers
400 Blue River Parkway
Silverthorne, Colorado 80498
Phone: 970-262-2878 or 888-876-8818
Fax: 970 262-2892
Web site: www.FishColorado.com

Edgewood Tahoe
180 Lake Parkway
Stateline, Nevada 89449
Phone: 775-588-3566
Fax: 775-588-8049
Reservations: 888-881-8659
Web site: www.Edgewood-Tahoe.com
Course Architect: George Fazio and
Tom Fazio

Fiji Sheraton Royal Denarau
P.O. Box 9081
Nadi, Fiji Islands
Phone: 679-750-000
Fax: 679-750-279
Reservations: 800-325-3535
Course: Denarau Golf & Racquet Club

Fiji Islands– Air Pacific Airlines
Reservations: 800-227-4446
Fax: 310-524-9356
Web site: www.AirPacific.com

Fiji Islands– Turtle Airway
Fiji float plane service
Phone: 679-722-389
Fax: 679-720-346

Four Seasons Resort Aviara
7100 Four Seasons Point
Carlsbad, California 92009
Phone: 760-603-6800
Fax: 790-603-6801
Reservations: 800-332-3442

Web site: www.FourSeasons.com
Golf Course: Aviara Golf Club
Phone: 760-603-6900
Course Architect: Arnold Palmer

Four Seasons Resort Bali
Jimbaran, Denpasar 80361
Bali, Indonesia
Phone: 62-361-701010
Fax: 62-361-701020

Grand Hyatt Bali
P.O. Box 53
Nusa Dua, Bali, Indonesia
Phone: 62-361-771234
Fax: 62-361-772038

Hilton Waikoloa Village
425 Waikoloa Beach Drive
Waikoloa, Hawaii 96738
Phone: 808-886-1234
Fax: 808-886-2900
Reservations: 800-Hiltons
Web site: www.Hilton.com
Golf Courses: Waikoloa Beach Course
and Kings Course
Course Architects: Robert Trent Jones
Jr. and Tom Weiskopf/Jay Morrish

Hokuli'a
78-6831 Ali'i Drive #K15
Kailua-Kona, Hawaii 96740
Phone: 808-324-6500
888-817-0833
Web site: www.Hokulia.com
Course Architect: Jack Nicklaus

Ko'olau Golf Club
45-550 Kionaole Road
Kaneohe, Oahu, HI 96744
Phone: 808-247-7088
Reservations: 808-236-4653
Web site: Koolau.AmericanGolf.com

Landmark Golf Club
84-000 Landmark Parkway
Indio, California 92203
Phone: 760-775-2000
Fax: 760-775-1988
Web site: www.LandmarkGC.com
Golf Courses: Skins North Course
and Skins South Course
Course Architect: Landmark Golf
Company and Schmidt-Curley Design

Lost Canyons Golf Club
3301 Lost Canyons Drive
Simi Valley, California 93063
Phone: 805-522-4653
Fax: 805-522-1389
Web site: www.LostCanyons.com
Golf Courses: Shadow Course and
Sky Course
Course Architects: Pete Dye and
Fred Couples

Marriott's Canyon Villas
5350 East Marriott Drive
Phoenix, Arizona 85054
Phone: 877-226-9663
Fax: 480-293-3870
Golf Courses: Wildfire Palmer Course
and Wildfire Faldo Course
Course Architects: Arnold Palmer
and Nick Faldo

**Marriott's Desert Springs
Resort & Spa**
74855 Country Club Drive
Palm Desert, California 92260
Phone: 760-341-2211
Fax: 760-341-1872
Reservations: 800-331-3112
Web site: DesertSpringsResort.com
Golf Courses: Palm & Valley
Course Architect: Ted Robinson

Marriott Grand Residence Club
1001 Park Avenue
South Lake Tahoe, California 96150
For Ownership: 866-20-GRAND
Fax: 530-542-6707
Reservations: 800-Villas-9
Web site: GrandResidenceClub.com

Marriott's Newport Coast Villas
23000 Newport Coast Drive
Newport Coast, California 92657
Phone: 888-765-3575
Web site: www.VacationClub.com

Marriott's Shadow Ridge
9000 Shadow Ridge Road
Palm Desert, California 92211
Villa Sales: 760-674-2800
Fax: 760-674-2810
Reservations: 760-674-2600
Golf Course: 760-674-2700
Course Architect: Nick Faldo

Marriott's Timber Lodge
4100 Lake Tahoe Boulevard
South Lake Tahoe, California 96150
For Ownership: 877-22-Tahoe
Fax: 530-542-6707
Reservations: 800-Villas-9
Web site: www.VacationClub.com

Pebble Beach Golf Links
1700 17 Mile Drive
Pebble Beach, California 93953
Phone: 800-654-9300
Web site: www.PebbleBeach.com
Course Architects: Jack Neville
Reservations: 800-654-9300

Pelican Hill Golf Club
22651 Pelican Hill Road South
Newport Coast, California 92657
Phone: 949-760-0707
Fax: 949-640-0855
Web site: www.PelicanHill.com
Golf Courses: Ocean North Course
and Ocean South Course
Course Architect: Tom Fazio

Rancho San Marcos Golf Course
4600 Highway 154
Santa Barbara, California 93105
Phone: 805-683-6334
Fax: 805-692-8805
Reservations: 877-RSM-1804
Web site: www.RSM1804.com
Course Architect: Robert Trent Jones, Jr.

Raven Golf Club at South Mountain
3636 East Baseline Road
Phoenix, Arizona 85040
Phone: 602-243-3636
Web site: www.RavenGolf.com
Course Architects: David Graham
and Gary Panks

Raven Golf Club at Three Peaks
2929 Eagle Road
Silverthorne, Colorado 80498
Phone: 970-262-3636
Fax: 970-262-6319
Reservations: 800-267-1650
Web site: www.3PKS.com
Course Architects: Tom Lehman and
Hurdzan-Fry Golf Design
Director of Golf: Rick Fretland

Resort at Squaw Creek
400 Squaw Creek Road
Olympic Valley, California 96146
Phone: 530 583-6300
Fax: 530-581-6632
Reservations: 800-403-4434
Web site: www.SquawCreek.com
Course Architect: Robert Trent Jones, Jr.
Airport: Reno/Tahoe International
Mountain High Balloons:
Phone: 530-587-6922
Reservations: 888-GO-ABOVE

Roaring Fork Club
100 Arbaney Ranch Road
Basalt, Colorado 81621
Phone: 970-927-9000
Fax: 970-927-2834
Web site: www.RoaringForkClub.net
Course Architect: Jack Nicklaus
Nearest Airport: Aspen, Colorado

Robinson Ranch Golf Club
27734 Sand Canyon Road
Santa Clarita, California 91351
Phone: 661-252-8484
Fax: 661-252-0001
Reservations: 661-252-7666
Web site: RobinsonRanchGolf.com
Golf Courses: Mountain Course and
Valley Course
Course Architect: Ted Robinson

Silverleaf
9255 East Desert Camp Drive
Scottsdale, Arizona 85255
Phone: 480-502-6902
Fax: 480-502-6903
Membership office: 480-502-6905
Golf Course: The Silverleaf Club
Web site: www.Silverleaf.com
Course Architect: Tom Weiskopf

**Superstition Mountain Golf and
Country Club**
3976 South Ponderosa Drive
Superstition Mountain, Arizona 85218
Phone: 877-983-3300
Fax: 480-983-3500
Web site: SuperstitionMountain.com
Golf Courses: Lost Gold course and
Prospector course
Course Architect: Nicklaus Design

The Highlands at Breckenridge
0069 Marksberry Way Drawer 8029
Breckenridge, Colorado 80424
Phone: 970-453-6900
Fax: 970-453-7900
Web site: HighlandsAtBreck.com
Course Architect: Jack Nicklaus

The Rim Golf Club
300 South Clubhouse Road
Payson, Arizona 85541
Phone: 928-474-1222
Fax: 928-472-8900
Web site: www.TheRimGolfClub.com
Course Architect: Tom Weiskopf and
Jay Morrish

Turtle Bay Resort
57-091 Kamehameha Highway
Kahuku, Oahu, Hawaii 96731
Phone: 808-293-8811
Fax: 808-293-9147
Reservations: 800-203-3650
Web site: www.TurtleBayResort.com
Golf Courses: Arnold Palmer Course
and George Fazio Course

Vatulele Island Resort
P.O. Box 9936
Fiji Islands
Phone: 679-50-300
Reservations: 612-932-61055
Web site: www.Vatulele.com

Wolf Creek at Paradise Canyon
401 Paradise Parkway, Suite 50
Mesquite, Nevada 89027
Phone: 866-230-2120
Private Vacation Club: 702-345-2173
Sales: 866-332-3358
Fax: 702-345-2124
Web site: www.GolfWolfCreek.com
Course Architect: Dennis Rider

Following page: The par 3, 212 yard 7th hole
on the South Course of the Francis H. I'i Brown
Golf Courses at Mauna Lani Resort.